'Taking us in a series of snapshots from his birth in 1956 to his escape to university, Edric looks back on it all with the curiosity and amazement of a man returned from a long way away ... all of this is precisely rendered, all of it assessed, in a book that feels as rich and carefully observed as any one of Edric's historical novels'

SUNDAY TIMES

'Robert Edric is the pseudonym of Gary Edric Armitage, the highly prolific and award-winning author of a shelf-load of novels. This hypnotic memoir is his first work of non-fiction and a remarkable piece of writing it is ... what any reader will take from this book is the mesmerising detail of daily life: the easy comradeship of fishing in the waters that speckle Sheffield; the happy organisation of life in the Cubs; the wider family such as racy Aunt Gloria, riding pillion on her boyfriend's motorbike, or beautiful, clever Aunt Mary, happily married with two young children, tragically stricken with cancer at 27'

DAILY MAIL BOOK OF THE WEEK

'This terrific account of Edric's working-class childhood in Sheffield – told as a series of snapshots that take in everything from the local working men's club to his utter contempt for his father – brilliantly fixes in the mind a time and a place that are now both utterly lost'

THE TIMES

'Tense and vivid ... each short, fluent chapter provides a pen portrait of family members, rituals, happenings, violent enmities and uneasy community ties, under a fug of beer and cigarette smoke'

TLS

'This is the first time Edric, who is best known as a novelist, has written autobiography, and his approach is singular. *My Own Worst Enemy* reads like a kind of inventory, each short chapter devoted to one aspect of working-class life in Sheffield in the 1960s … The detail is incredible, a film running before the reader's eyes. Whether he is describing an onyx cigarette lighter or a spinning leather chair, you realise all that you have forgotten, but he has not, and you feel both grateful and just a little alarmed'

OBSERVER

'A painfully honest, almost Orwellian account of a struggling family expected to meet the every need of their demanding father, who never lets them forget that he deserved better in life'

THE TABLET

'Held me rapt … Edric's hyper-precise detailing of his working-class Sheffield childhood and appalling father is utterly compelling'

PATRICK GALE

MY
OWN
WORST
ENEMY

ROBERT
EDRIC

SCENES
OF A
CHILDHOOD

Swift

SWIFT PRESS

This paperback edition first published by Swift Press 2022
First published in Great Britain by Shoestring Press 2020

1 3 5 7 9 10 8 6 4 2

Copyright © Robert Edric 2020

The right of Robert Edric to be identified as the author of this work has been
asserted in accordance with the Copyright, Designs and Patents Act 1988.

Text designed and set in Minion by Tetragon, London
Printed and bound in Great Britain by CPI Group (UK) Ltd, Croydon, CR0 4YY

A CIP catalogue record for this book is available from the British Library

ISBN: 978-1-80075-083-8
eISBN: 978-1-80075-082-1

for Gloria, Joan A, Joan R, Mary, Teresa & Valerie

1

ONE afternoon, when I was twelve years old and had recently started at grammar school, I came home at half past four to find both my mother and my father already there. This was unsettlingly unusual: ten to six was my father's regular return from work, my mother having arrived a frantic quarter of an hour earlier to prepare the cooked meal he expected to be awaiting him.

All of us in that small house were acutely aware of my father's comings and goings, of the shadows he cast, but what made this particular occasion even more unnerving was the fact that he was now sitting in his usual place – *his* chair, beside the fire facing the television – wearing an all-too-obvious wig to cover his balding head. He was still a young man – thirty-four or -five – but his hair was already half lost, leaving a thin, carefully configured wreath above his ears and across the back of his head. The few longer strands of hair were combed over the top, and everything was held in place with hair spray. The vivid scarlet and black of his Cossack aerosol can was decorated with the outline of a horseman – a Cossack, presumably – wearing busby-like headwear and brandishing a curved sabre. The smell and residue of the spray filled the small kitchen where my father prepared himself before his equally punctual departure at half past seven to one or other of the pubs he frequented most nights of the week.

My mother, a year younger, sat beside him, avoiding looking at his head, and both of them watched me closely as I came into the room. Naturally, I wanted to know why the pair of them were home at that earlier time and what this sudden drama of the wig meant.

My father was a vain, self-regarding man, endlessly preening and combing and brushing and checking his appearance; but even for him this seemed an excessive and ridiculous – ridiculously *public* – step to have taken. Both of them continued watching me, waiting for me to speak, causing me to become even more cautious with my response. My father would argue black was white, and my mother usually encouraged everyone present – more often than not myself, my younger sister and brother – to go along with this to prevent any further anger on his part.

I finally said something noncommittal, like, I can see something's different.

This seemed to work, briefly.

It's your dad's new haircut, my mother said tentatively. He's had it styled differently, something more modern.

Styled. Even the word and all it implied added another edge to the exchange. Nothing about that household or the five people in it was ever *styled*.

But even this clearly untrue explanation left me wondering. Whatever *they* might have wanted me to believe, it was still all too obviously a wig. The hair immediately above his ears was pale and greying, and while there was clearly some attempt to blend the artificial with what remained of the real, the join, like everything else, was glaringly evident. The new, flatter covering over the top of my father's head was now a shiny, almost gingery colour.

Then my father broke the spell of uncertainty which held all three of us and said, He can see I've not had it cut different. Give the lad some credit. It's a toupee.

That's right. Not a wig, my mother added quickly, almost as though between them they had been trying to trick me.

It's real hair, my father said, almost proudly. Human hair. Styled and fitted to match his own hair precisely, and coloured to blend seamlessly with what little of that hair he still possessed.

In my usual evasive, compliant way, I looked more closely and told him you could hardly tell.

Of course you can't, he said. That's the difference between a toupee and an ordinary wig.

I wondered if I was expected to reach out and feel it. I rarely went too close to my father, none of us did.

Only then, wondering what to say next, did it occur to me that, apart from my mother and whoever had created and then fitted the contraption to my father's head, I was the first to witness this transformation.

You can hardly see the difference, I said again, pretending to search for the invisible seam.

I sensed even then, at that young age, that this was the great paradox, burden and fear of all wig-wearers, and especially male wig-wearers: that everyone, absolutely, positively everyone – even those people who had never known or seen you pre-wig – knew that you were wearing a wig. The wig-wearer was compromised and the person who knew it was a wig was doubly compromised. Whatever happened – whatever conversation or exchange now took place in my father's life – everything would be overridden by those styled, pale gingery hairs sitting on his head. Whereas before, his vanity had been something those around him had taken for granted and either tolerated or ignored, now it shouted out at them every time he appeared and as they tried not to let their amused gaze wander above his eyes.

It's called a Crown Topper, he said. He showed me a brochure that had been hidden beneath the newspaper on the floor beside him.

The glossy pages showed Before and After photos of once-bald and now-toupeed men. And on not a single one of them did their new head of hair look any more natural or any less obvious or ridiculous than it now did on my father.

It's called a weave, my mother said. Every single hair, and there are hundreds—

Thousands, my father corrected her.

Thousands. And every single one of them has been put in place by hand and then cut and styled to look like that. My mother, I knew, was as wary and as fearful of her own part in the exchange as I was. I could hardly remember having had a normal conversation with my father before, let alone one as momentous and as dangerous as this.

Knowing some further admiring or encouraging response was being prompted, I asked him how it stayed on his head, and before answering me, he took hold of the hair at the crown of his head and peeled it slowly forward, flinching at the slight tug of the adhesive tape which held it in place. This tape, he explained to me, came in a roll, like Sellotape, but was double-sided, to be cut freshly and applied daily. He continued rolling the hair forward until the flimsy scalp sat in his hand. He held this out to me.

You can feel it, my mother said, as though this might help.

I touched if for a respectable second or two and then drew back my hand. I was more impressed by the fact that you could get *double*-sided adhesive tape.

Every six months I have an appointment to go to the Crown Topper *agent* to see if anything needs altering, my father said. All part of the *Executive Service*.

I wondered what he meant. Did he mean the hair would grow?

Colouring, my mother said. It keeps everything looking natural. Everything's properly done. By experts. It's not cheap.

For my mother, the lack of money in our household was a constant and worrying concern, something to be scrupulously controlled on a weekly, often daily basis. The wig – toupee – I was then told, had cost hundreds of pounds. I was expected to be impressed by this and so I let out a long, admiring breath and nodded slowly. My father, I knew, and despite his endless quest after Life's bargains and knock-down prices, would regard the expense as a further guarantee of the wig's quality.

I had started learning French only months earlier. Above the first 'e' of the word toupée was an accent, and I knew what that accent was called and what it signified. I knew what they were *all* called and what they *all* signified. I resisted showing off this cleverness in front of my father, but I knew that this additional, exotic, unnecessary extra would also have appealed to him. Just as it would have appealed to all those other men trying desperately to avoid using the word wig or hairpiece.

I went on nodding at everything the pair of them told me, wondering if either of *them* was convinced by this all-too-clearly rehearsed delivery. But even as I considered this, I remember feeling a vague sense of satisfaction in the knowledge that this side of his nature – his vanity and self-regard at the expense of his family – was now unavoidably and blatantly revealed to everyone else. It was unlikely that most of those others – family, workmates and drinking friends – weren't already aware of my father's nature, but at least now it was an undeniable fact, and one, in my own young mind at least, upon which our endless further conflicts might hinge and then be silently, albeit often tearfully and painfully, won.

My mother said something more about the toupee already making him look younger, knocking years off him. In contrast to the time and care my father took over himself, *she* had long since stopped paying attention to her own appearance, and had started to gain the weight which she would continue to carry for the rest of her life.

It also occurred to me on that awkward afternoon that few others would be as generous in their silence or feigned admiration of the toupee as she or I were being then. Others, I knew, would be only too happy to point out to him that he was wearing a wig. Worse, perhaps – they would keep their scorn, ridicule and amusement to themselves and then laugh at him behind his back.

He asked my mother to help him put the toupee back in place. A new circular, magnifying mirror and slender, tapering metal comb were produced. These, along with the double-sided tape, were all part of the Crown Topper Executive After-Care Package. As was the equally impressive polystyrene dummy's head already sitting on the dressing table in their bedroom, upon which the sacred toupee would now sit and keep its shape overnight.

My mother smoothed the woven hair back into place and my father pushed its edges back into his thinning strands with the narrow end of the comb.

See how easy it is? he said. Wigs are nothing but trouble, but this…

I nodded. I was still in my new and uncomfortable school uniform with my stiff, heavy leather satchel at my feet. I began to resent the fact that he was home so early, that the precious time before his own usual reappearance in the house had been lost to me.

I wondered if I was now expected to pass on to my sister and brother, three and six years younger, everything that had just happened. Despite my growing awareness of what the wearing of the wig would come to mean to us all, I could not imagine what a terrible prospect faced my parents as this supposedly transformed man now presented himself anew to the world. I could certainly have had no idea then of the lies, evasions and other strategies the pair of them were already being forced to consider. And I gave no thought whatsoever to my father's own understanding of himself, or to how this might now change his standing in the eyes of that watching world. And even if I *had* been able to imagine any of these things, I doubt I would have cared or sympathized with the man. One of the things I *was* able to consider, however, was the understanding that we, his family, would all now be expected to play our part in the deceits and subterfuges which lay ahead of us.

I doubt if any of us truly understood then what an explosive charge had been placed at our centre. The visible could never be made invisible again. People who looked at him might remain polite or pretend not to see, but what would happen when the first of them – provoked, perhaps, by my father's own provocations – pointed to the toupee and said, It's a wig. What then? What argument based on honesty or sincerity or openness was a man wearing a wig ever going to win? Even the knowledge of what the wig had cost – and would continue to cost if the Crown Topper programme was to be adhered to – would be a cause for finger-pointing or that same behind-hand mockery.

I learned soon afterwards that, following an initial consultation and down-payment, my father had signed yet another hire-purchase agreement and was buying his toupee – or, rather, toupees, as it turned out – on credit that we as a family could ill afford.

The polystyrene head was of as much interest to me as the wig itself. It was clearly a woman's head, vividly white, egg-shaped and smooth, with only nominal eyes, nose and lips. The men in the glossy brochure were manly men, with cigarettes, golf clubs and sports cars, and with attractive, fashionably dressed young women on their arms.

When, finally, there was nothing more to be imparted concerning the wig, I was ushered upstairs to change out of my school uniform and to get started on my homework in the bedroom I shared with my young brother, looking out over the terrace of houses opposite.

Later, examining the polystyrene head, I wanted to finally laugh and to shout out loud that it was a fucking wig, that it was all too fucking obviously a fucking wig, and that soon the whole fucking world would know and finally see my father for exactly what he fucking well was. Soon everybody in the whole fucking world would be pointing at him and laughing at him. But all this was tempered by the understanding that those same people might then smirk and whisper to each other and point surreptitiously at the rest of us, puzzled, perhaps, by our collective complicity in pretending that nothing whatsoever had happened. Besides, it was a small house, and anyone shouting in any of its few small rooms would be clearly heard in all the others.

The grammar school had given me a homework timetable – three subjects, half an hour each, four nights a week; three hours every weekend. I was an organized child and I liked to get everything done – it usually took me no more than an hour – before making my tea. This was invariably followed by an hour of television before my father's return from work. The drama of the revelation of the toupee had already upset this routine, knocking me off schedule, making me late.

2

I WAS delivered at Sheffield Children's hospital, Jessop's, in April 1956. I was told that I was born on the stroke of midnight between Friday the thirteenth and Saturday the fourteenth and that consequently my mother was given the choice of dates to put on my birth certificate. Being a superstitious woman, she naturally chose the latter. I was also told that because of these portentous circumstances, my eyes always shone red in photographs.

Mostly our few photographs were formal and carefully posed, full of grimaces and fixed smiles and taken only on special occasions such as annual holidays and Christmas. The majority of them were black and white, small and with serrated borders. There was no indication of my alleged red-eye look until the instant, flashbulb-lit Polaroids of my later childhood. My mother, then and ever after, always favoured the more melodramatic interpretation over the scientific, prosaic or rational. If there *was* intended to be something of the supernatural about my midnight birth, then as a young boy I understood and secretly appreciated the obviously demonic aspect of this.

As with many women of her generation, class and upbringing, my mother believed in what was broadly and enthusiastically regarded as the supernatural. Horoscopes were consulted and believed; séances, private and public, were a common entertainment, as were tarot, palm and tea leaf readings. Every family story demanded and was given its drama, its edge and its inexplicable elements.

My father mocked all this. He told his wife she was descended from gypsies – gyppos. He needed no further proof of this than her lustrous jet-black hair and her dark complexion. Her maiden name was Gregory. There had been a Pope Gregory, and so in all likelihood she was probably descended from Catholics, too. And everyone knew that all gyppos were Catholics. And everyone knew what Catholics were like when *they* were at home. Partly, I suspect, some part of my mother's cherished melodramatic self appreciated this shadowy, unproven and romanticized background. The women she visited in their booths at the seaside had the same dark hair and skin. Their brightly coloured headscarves were pulled tighter to their heads and their bracelets, earrings and necklaces might have been gaudier, but, essentially, the similarities were obvious and the comparisons were there to be made and savoured.

As a child it was difficult for me to understand the true nature or source of my father's humiliation and mockery of his wife, but it was an unmistakeable and ever-present fact of their life together. Sometimes it almost seemed a kind of affection between them – the only sort he might easily or openly express. At other times it was clearly the undisguised public expression of his frustration and anger at the way his own life had turned out. He was, essentially, a bully, and, as with all bullies, there always needed to be a target in sight, always a dependency or weakness needing to be exploited or punished.

Everything was a competition with my father, everything a judgement concluded by a condemnation. His anger at the world, and at his own unhappy place in it, seemed never to find a proper or positive focus and so it was cast around indiscriminately, serving a purpose only he truly appreciated.

I learned twenty-five years later, on the occasion of my parents' silver wedding anniversary, that I was born six months after they were married, and that my mother's pregnancy had led directly to that momentous event in their two young lives.

My mother, in her angriest moments – perhaps finally understanding all that she had forsaken in marrying this scornful, restless and resentful man, and subjugating herself entirely to him and bearing him two more children – would tell the story of how her prospective mother-in-law had warned her against marrying her own son. It was in his nature, my mother was told, to demean and to belittle, to make anyone close to him as unsettled and as unhappy as he was. But what choice then did my mother have? I doubt either of them did not have great hopes of their future together after all they had both been through in recent years.

There are those small black and white photos of the pair of them together before my arrival in which my mother looks the image of Audrey Hepburn. Slim, shapely, dark-haired and large-eyed, and in close-fitting dresses and blouses and slacks which showed off her figure and all-to-obvious appeal. Her lips are richly made up, perhaps because of her dark colouring. In some of the photos, my father, his white shirt tucked into his narrow and tightly belted waist, stares at her smiling with an intense affection that few ever saw afterwards.

He did his National Service between the ages of eighteen and twenty, part of it in Egypt. I was frequently referred to as a Suez Baby, and this, like my supposedly auspicious arrival, I also appreciated.

My father's mother died eighteen months after my birth, aged forty-five. His father had died long before I was born, at the age of thirty-eight. Upon the death of his mother, the six children of the family – the eldest boy twenty-five, the youngest girl only thirteen – were left together in the council house into which the family had moved before the war. This created relationships and bonds – brothers and sisters turned parents and children – which, to begin with at least, served them all well. Perhaps, too, it was this that helped steer my youthful parents toward their marriage – a marriage in which my father insisted on using his own upbringing as a template both for treating his wife and for raising his own three children.

There is a solitary photo of me as a baby with my maternal grandmother, chubby – bonny, people would have said, meaning fat and healthy – barely upright on sausage legs, made even chubbier-looking by my hand-knitted baby clothes and waterproof pants over a nappy, short socks and bootees. My grandmother – though I never knew her as such – is standing over me, leaning forward, holding my shoulders, keeping me upright and facing the camera. In one hand I am holding the stem of a rose bush. I am looking anxious, ready to fall. My hair is vividly blond – soon to darken – and I am dressed in white from head to toe. Prominent at my grandmother's throat is a large crucifix, dangling free of her blouse collar and cardigan. Her face is thin and drawn, though she seems genuinely happy to be holding her first grandchild in the front garden of the family home like that. Everything about the photograph yells Occasion.

The woman died soon afterwards, and perhaps she and everyone else around her knew she was dying when the photo was taken. Perhaps that was *why* it was taken. The picture was enlarged and then made permanent inside a glass and gilt frame with a hinged wooden stand suggesting it was meant to be displayed. We were not a family of photographic history – the odd and obligatory school photo here and there, perhaps – and this solitary picture of the baby and the old, dying woman always struck me as one of a kind.

I'd like to believe that my father himself took the photo and that his dying mother appreciated this connection with me before that short-lived, fragile bond was lost for ever.

If I sound intrigued and moved by the picture, then these are only recent sensations experienced upon looking at it now. Growing up, I knew neither the woman's name nor that of her lost husband – Lillian and Norman – my paternal grandfather.

Curiously, I remember that the narrow path in the front garden of that council house was filled with clinker and lined with house bricks set into the earth at an angle to create a diamond pattern. In a world of coking plants, steelworks and decade-old bomb sites still mounded with rubble, these were common features of tens of thousands of carefully tended small gardens.

The only other photograph of any consequence that survives of my first year of childhood is one of me posed sitting on a sideboard, again clean and smartly dressed and bulging in handmade clothes. As in the picture with my unknown grandmother, my hair is shockingly white and seems now to have been raised to a central crest. I am still chubby and grinning, my arms and legs and cheeks still full and round.

I appear to be clutching the edge of the sideboard, about to propel myself forward.

It was only eleven years after the end of the war; newborns still routinely died in their first months, and I have always considered this picture to be a kind of recognition that I had survived and prospered. That there was something special about the picture is witnessed by the professional photographer's stamp on the back of the photo. Faded and unreadable now, only the word 'Studio' remains – more than enough.

I was a baby and child of the recently inaugurated National Health Service. The same one that had seen my young mother through her partially unwed pregnancy. The same service that, had it been available to them sooner, might have saved the lives of both my father's middle-aged parents, or at least have made the effort on their behalves.

In many of his arguments, my father would defeat his opponents by shouting at them that they had no idea what it was like to have lost both parents at such a young age. He resented the ease and comfort and certainty in the lives of others when in his own young life there had been only hardship, loss and struggle.

It was another of his argument-winning gambits to announce to us all that we didn't know we were born and that, by comparison with his own childhood, everything in our young lives was handed to us on a plate, and for which we showed not the slightest bit of gratitude. There was a roof over our heads and always food on the table – two things *he* had never been certain of as a child. What more could we possibly want? And on the occasions when his anger curdled to violence, he would tell us that we should be grateful to him for only using his hands to teach us our lessons; his own father, he said, would have taken his belt off long before now.

Whenever my mother grew angry at us in his absence, her final, most potent rebuke was to tell us to wait until he got home when she would tell him of our bad behaviour. She seldom *did* tell him, of course, and her own affection for us was shaped and tempered as much by her husband's predictable responses as by her own true feelings for her children. We all understood this, and while she did occasionally resort to proper punishments – slapping and banishments – they were, we felt, deserved and fairly administered only as a last resort.

She often told us that she was at the end of her tether, that we were driving her into an early grave. She saved her favourite pay-off – You'll be sorry when I'm dead; where will you all be then? – for when the argument was over and we were already feeling remorse for having upset her.

My father was one of six – Ray, Valerie, himself, Gloria, Tony and Mary. Three boys, three girls, all of them bound together and dependent on the others by force of hard circumstance. It proved a difficult arrangement from which to extricate themselves as individuals when the time came, and especially when other wives and husbands and children eventually came along.

My mother was one of two. She met my father when she was fourteen or fifteen. He was her only boyfriend, then fiancé, then husband, then father to her children. Her sister, Joan, was a year older, and as girls they looked like twins, sharing the same good looks and dark features. In the photographs of the pair of them together they strike me as two halves of the same person. There is something both alluring and mischievous about the way they sit on a wall together, their arms and legs bare and their hair and faces carefully brushed and made up for the camera. There is also a confident, shameless, knowing quality to the girl my mother had once been that did not long survive the marriage into which she, still a teenager, may already have been drifting as the poses were being struck.

3

DEEMING it both old-fashioned and too much like hard work every morning, my father blocked up our coal fire. No more sacks of coal tipped into the cellar and filling the house with its dust. No more sooty lines and shadows along the picture rail and thin skirting. And instead of the messy, ash and clutter-filled open hearth, we now possessed a clean and efficient – and *modern* – gas fire.

A wooden surround was quickly added, upon which my mother displayed her few knick-knacks, pottery and glass figures – *figurines* – the odd piece of onyx or crystal. Moulded golden plastic tiles formed a backing to this. The peeling mural of the Canadian Rockies which had filled the wall above the old fireplace upon our arrival in the house was replaced by a three-dimensional wall of plastic pebbles in grey, black and white, exactly like the pebbles on a beach, but in a repeating pattern which was disappointingly obvious, and whose rounded edges seldom matched up. It was a *feature* wall, my father said. Who else did we know who possessed a feature wall? Nobody, that's who.

On either side of the chimney breast, in narrow alcoves, my father stuck up two more of the golden tiles. He'd bought too many in the first place and it would have been a crying shame not to have used them; they didn't come cheap. The golden theme was completed by an Aztec-like sundial on one wall and by a precious golden carriage clock placed at the centre of the mantel above the new fire and its dazzling surround.

The carriage clock was always considered to be the most valuable and precious object we possessed. It had glass sides, revealing its intricate workings, claw legs, a black and white dial with Roman numerals, and a golden dome surmounted by an ornamental spire. It looked old, antique, but wasn't; the box of such a precious thing was precious in itself and deemed worthy of saving on the top of a wardrobe. It would come in handy if ever we moved house again, which was unlikely. Besides, even if the clock wasn't an actual antique, then the chances were it would soon become one. The word heirloom was used.

When anyone moved too close to the new fire – and who would be so selfish as to block everyone else's heat? – we were warned to watch the clock. My father listened for the time signal on the radio and adjusted the delicate hands accordingly. Not that this needed doing. Accurate to within a second a year was the manufacturer's proud and unlikely boast – as though that carefully regulated second might one day be of some great value to someone. But the greatest gift of that second was the opportunity it forever gave my father to ask the infrequent visitors to our house to guess how much time the clock lost in a year. When I once suggested that the second might be gained rather than lost over the year, my ignorance was laughed at. I was told – was *forever* being told – to stick to what little I did actually know about and to leave the rest to the experts. And if there were no experts present – meaning my father – then I was to defer to anyone older than me – again, usually my father.

When my mother dusted the clock she held it firmly in place and screwed her yellow duster to a point. It was a fiddly thing to keep clean. On the rare occasion the clock was actually polished – little need now that we had forsaken coal for gas – the task was undertaken as though it were a fraught and complicated piece of surgery.

To complete the modernization of our living room, in which all five of us could sit within easy reach of each other and the television controls, my father replaced the door between this room and the kitchen with a plastic folding screen – a door which concertinaed open and shut, and through which a cold draught always blew. This lasted a few years before being replaced in turn by a pair of highly varnished, chest-high, swinging doors. Just like the bar-room doors John Wayne swaggered through to get into his saloons and order his tiny glasses of whisky before someone started a fight with him and the whole bar erupted into choreographed violence and lively music. These left even more open space between the living room and the kitchen and the draught was correspondingly greater.

All repair and maintenance work in the house was undertaken by my father. Because who in their right mind would employ a professional builder or plumber or decorator or electrician and pay a small fortune for the privilege when anything that needed doing was usually just common sense anyway? And certainly nobody ever needed a window cleaner or drain unblocker or hedge- or lawn-cutter. A man cleared his own gutters and drains, cut his own lawns and hedges. He borrowed ladders and climbed up onto his own roof to fix the inevitable few loose slates when they started letting in water. And who even bothered with the odd rattling chimney pot or sagging aerial?

Our old sash windows were replaced with windows featuring adjustable *louvres* through which both the rain and the wind slowly seeped.

We acquired a large black leather-effect chair which cupped whoever sat in it, and which spun on its stand. My father sat in it like a judge in his court and warned the rest of us about using it. The chair was too large for the small room and blocked the door to the cellar head, where my mother stored her cans of food. The spinning chair was not a thing to play with. Wear and tear. In addition to spinning, the chair also tilted back and forth slightly, making it even more irresistible to us in his absence. A leather footstool completed the set. What more could a man ask for after a hard day's work than to sit back and relax in his own home, in front of the television, with an ashtray on a stand close beside him, and with the ability to both recline slightly and to simultaneously swivel from side to side?

And then the black and white television was replaced by a much larger, colour set. People, places and events were revealed to us for the first time just as they looked in real life. The new television came in its own pale cabinet – veneer, but who was counting? – with slatted doors that slid open and shut in a curve. My mother put more of her ornaments on the narrow shelf at the base of the screen.

We acquired a circular glass-topped coffee table which fitted as awkwardly as the spinning chair into the small room, upon which was placed a three-tiered 'humidifier' – three plastic bowls connected to a bubbling waterfall. Plastic lilies floated in the largest bowl and the sound of gently bubbling water competed with the television.

Opposite the wall of plastic pebbles, more varnished wooden cladding appeared. Wall lights in the shape of Chinese lanterns were added, illuminated by dim red bulbs. A lava lamp was positioned on the television, and its floating fluorescent waxy blobs were never less than a distraction.

We were a household desperate to move forward, to leave the hard times of my parents' own childhoods behind. My father frequently reminded us of how lucky we were to be the wife and children of a man with such vision and taste. His brothers and sisters – all those old-fashioned slum- and council-house-dwelling relatives – were stuck in the past and being left far behind us, as my father – and he alone – revealed himself to be one of those men with their fingers constantly on the pulse and their eyes fixed on the main chance directly ahead of them.

A further shelf was fitted to one of the alcoves and an eight-track cartridge player and six or seven cartridges were proudly displayed – Gilbert O'Sullivan, Andy Williams, Barbara Streisand, *The Best of Yorkshire Brass Bands*.

A bookcase appeared in the opposite alcove and what few books the house contained – Reader's Digest volumes and the occasional Catherine Cookson – were lined up along its broad shelves. And not just any old shelving – *adjustable* shelving that could be moved up and down on plastic pegs depending on the size of your books and whatever other displayable knick-knacks you possessed. Ingenious.

4

I SPENT my first six years in the village of Ecclesfield on the
northern outskirts of Sheffield, and toward which, from
the end of the Great War onward, a vast council estate, Parson
Cross, was already spreading, burying every field and copse
beneath roads and houses, and leaving only the narrow flood-
plains of a few streams as any indicator of what had existed
before. The garden in which I was posed with my unknown
grandmother was on this estate. Trees were planted along the
broader roads, and people were proud of their new homes.
Corner shops, newsagents, bookies, greengrocers, chip shops
and pubs were planted on avenues and crescents at regular
intervals among the spreading houses.

Most of my wider family ended up on the estate one way or
another. But not us. When I was six, we moved in the opposite direction, away from semi-rural Ecclesfield toward the
cramped streets and industries of the city centre.

Buses connected Ecclesfield with that city centre, but these
were infrequent and did not run on Sundays. Vast, millstone
chapels stood on most of the main streets, mostly Methodist,
but other, rarer sects too.

Along the valley bottom, amid scattered patches of untended
woodland and slowly settling slag heaps, there were forges,

mills and a coking plant, all of which pumped smoke and steam into the air and which made the sky glow at night. The beating of distant machinery could almost always be heard. A few local pits remained in operation, and it was evident everywhere that this had once been an industrial landscape. Despite the fields and woodlands and reed-fringed ponds, this was still coal and steel country.

Apart from brick, anything of any substance in the village was built of soft sandstone which quickly blackened in the sooty air, and which turned back to sand when rubbed vigorously. Failing farms and smallholdings sat amid the houses and factories; allotments with their ramshackle sheds and greenhouses abutted the high wire fencing of the factories and works.

Over a wall from the L-shaped court where I spent those first six years was a small pig farm, each creature and its litter contained in narrow concrete pens. The farmer collected food waste from the local schools and factory canteens and scooped this from galvanized buckets to feed the animals. The smell and the noise of the pigs were ever present, and people knew hourly which way the wind was blowing.

My parents moved from their parental homes into a two-up, two-down, gardenless house built around a tarmacked courtyard, at the centre of which stood a line of three toilets serving a dozen houses. The front door of our house opened onto a small patch of wasteland, the rear onto the yard and the toilets. Next to the house was a tunnel which led into the yard, and beyond this, on the corner of the court, stood a small grocer's shop, where almost everything required was bought on a daily basis as needed.

Inside, the house comprised a single living room and an even smaller kitchen, in which sat a Formica-topped table and chairs. A shallow porcelain sink was served by a single cold tap. A gas cooker, upon which all water was heated, completed the kitchen.

In good weather, the yard outside was filled with housewives and playing children. It was a small but true community and I was happy there. Chairs and tin baths were frequently taken outside and children were bathed weekly and communally. Women contributed kettles of hot water. Children played naked and were guarded and cosseted by all present. Returning fathers brought sweets and whatever might be left in their snap tins. Men went out clean each morning and came home dirty. They washed at their cold water sinks and then came outside to smoke and to talk.

I attended the infant school directly across the street from my home. At the edge of the small playground there stood a corrugated iron air-raid shelter still haunted by the ghosts of all the children who had allegedly been killed there during the recent war.

One of the towering, solid chapels stood across the side road from the school, and beyond this the rapidly spreading housing estate continued to flow into every available and pre-viously bypassed piece of land. The roads of the estate were said to have been laid in concrete by Italian prisoners of war. People still spoke of the men. Few people possessed a car, but everyone spoke of the makeshift quality of these concrete roads when compared to those constructed by Sheffield City Council Highways Department. People remembered taking in the Italian labourers for meals and accompanying them to church and chapel on Sundays.

My mother's parents moved into a new house on the estate when their old one was finally demolished. A home with three downstairs and three upstairs rooms, an indoor toilet, a bath-room and a kitchen, and all for only two old people.

The house was fitted with carpets which reached to the walls, and which my house-proud grandmother covered with plastic pathways to keep clean. A cabinet in the front room contained our family's only complete china tea service, along with a tea pot, milk jug and sugar bowl of Sheffield plate, alleg-edly the next best thing to solid silver. A boiler was lit to fill the bath and, again weekly, my parents carried me and towels to the house, and we all bathed and then ate our tea there.

On one airless summer night in Ecclesfield there was a fire at the pig farm and all the pigs were killed. It is one of my first, lasting memories. People said that the noise made by the pigs as they perished was a terrible thing to hear. I remember as a four- or five-year-old being made to leave my bed and my home on that summer's night, and then afterwards standing and watching as the fire brigade arrived to douse the flames. Like all distant memories of childhood, my recollection of the drama of the burning pigs has become fixed in all its inaccu-racies and fictional embellishments.

It was the end of the farm and a big event in the village. The land was cleared and more houses were quickly built. Soon afterwards, our courtyard was infested by mice, dozens of which were discovered to be coming through a far wall, beneath which the women laid out their tin baths of water and bleach to catch and drown the creatures. Swarms of flies were often a problem, and flypapers hung from most ceilings, shiny and toffee-coloured and slowly filling with their trapped victims. These are all further vivid memories, isolated and clear amid forgotten years, and so they remain of some inexplicable importance to me.

Another grocer's elsewhere in the village would display plastic animals in a small side window. Sometimes farm animals, sometimes wild. The display changed every few weeks and had nothing whatsoever to do with the shop itself. Close by stood a disused mill dam in which men fished. The water was dark and reportedly of great depth. The land surrounding the dam was marshy and filled with dead and fallen trees. A narrow channel ran out of the pond at one end through a debris-clogged grill. Old men fished the water, members of a nearby working men's club, and once every hour or so a small silver fish was pulled out of the water and swung skilfully into a waiting palm. Mostly, the men were content simply to sit in silence on their wicker baskets, smoking, sipping from flasks and watching the vivid tips of their floats in the black water. Beyond the dam, up a slope occasionally filled with grazing cattle, stood the massive Saint Mary's church, where I was baptized, but which neither I nor my parents ever visited again. People in the family laughed and said we were all Godless.

And beyond the church, along rutted, gated paths lay the true countryside of wheat fields and woodland, century-old farms with their dilapidated outbuildings and ponds of their own. People saw foxes here, and deer moving in and out of the trees and over the flattened spoil heaps.

Looking back, everything about Ecclesfield and my first six contented years there seemed to exist in a kind of perfect yet threatened balance – everything I could ever need was there, all of it close to home, and yet all of it forever on the point of coming to an end.

5

Almost every adult I knew smoked, most continually, many heavily: twenty to forty cigarettes a day would be considered normal, sixty not unusual. My mother and father smoked, all my uncles and most of my aunts smoked. My grandmother and grandfather smoked. They all smoked like they drank their endless cups of tea – without thinking, because it was a cheap and simple pleasure, and because it was something to do when nothing else presented itself.

People smoked while they were eating, performing household chores, while on the toilet – especially while on the toilet; smoking was considered an aid to constipation. They smoked while shopping, in the cinema, driving, waiting for a bus. An evening watching television was completed only by a succession of boiled kettles and filled ashtrays. Perhaps no one noticed the smell of smoke which permeated the house and which impregnated clothes, carpets, furnishings, hair; certainly no one would ever be rude enough to mention it or, God forbid, to ask people to stop, however briefly. Occasionally, someone might jokingly ask for a window or door to be opened, or someone would use a folded newspaper to waft away the gathering smoke when the air finally became too thick.

When we still had the coal fire, the various streams of pale blue tobacco smoke could be seen flowing across the room toward the flames and the chimney's up-draught.

In addition to the ashtray on a pedestal beside my father's chair, others sat on every surface. A plunger at the top of the pedestal meant that both ash and stubs could be spun away out of sight into the hollow base of the stand. Another of our prize possessions, second only to the carriage clock, was a lighter embedded in a block of onyx four or five inches square. To us, the onyx was a precious stone. Other ashtrays came from pubs, advertising various drinks. Cigarette ends were extinguished and left beside uneaten food or dropped into half-filled mugs of cold tea, where they hissed and were left to disintegrate before the cup was retrieved, rinsed and used again. Outside, glowing tips were crushed between nicotine-stained fingers and thumbs and the dying sparks scattered to the ground.

Men who had been in the Navy – or so we imagined – smoked only Senior Service, strong, full-strength, filterless cigarettes. When these or the more common Park Drive were not available, those same men would snap off the filters of other brands and smoke these. Frugal men broke cigarettes in half and put part behind their ear for later. Packets were offered around as casually and as freely as greetings; people often took two cigarettes at a time and no one was offended.

Men brandished treasured lighters like trophies. My father possessed a small circular brass lighter with the crest of the Yorks and Lancs Regiment in which he had served his National Service. It had a wick and a metal flint and was fuelled by petrol. Most of these lighters were teased to life only by the men who knew how to operate them, and the flames from both these and struck matches were cupped in windbreak hands as men huddled together in a kind of conspiracy to reach the flame.

Chain-smokers lit their next cigarette from the glowing stub of their last. Some men held their fags in the hollow ball of their hands with the filter barely protruding from the circle of their yellow fingers and nails. Some men, my father included, occasionally kept their cigarettes in a slim gilt case, pulled from an inner pocket and then opened and a cigarette removed in a single deft, one-handed movement. When one of these was out, the case was then flicked shut and the cigarette ceremoniously tapped against its lid. Many of these cases had been received as gifts and were dutifully inscribed with the initials of the smoker.

My grandfather smoked a pipe, and like most men his age he carried a small Sheffield-made penknife with a miniature blade designed solely for clearing out the residue of the wooden bowl – a combination of resinous, half-burned tobacco and congealed, evaporated saliva. Each time it was lit, the pipe would be inspected, tapped against a hard surface and then scraped clean; or the surface of the remaining, unburned tobacco would be scraped and then supplemented with fresh strands. My grandfather's thumb fitted perfectly into the bowl and was used to press down this new tobacco.

Lighting the pipe was always another carefully observed ceremony – holding a lit match slightly above the bowl's rim and then making a succession of gentle sucks so that the flame flared and then bent down toward its waiting fuel. This was done three or four times until smoke was rising, after which any excess fire was smothered to a glow beneath the ball of a leathery thumb. Eventually, the spent match was waved out and the pipe considered up and running.

After that, it was a simple matter of knowing how often and how hard to suck on the stem. The bowl of the pipe was detachable for cleaning and every household possessed a packet of pipe cleaners – usually kept in a mug on the mantel – for this. Men blew into their detached stems and these whistled. Lifelong smokers made a great thing of favouring one brand or blend of tobacco over another.

Pavements and streets, especially around bus shelters and the entrance to public buildings, were strewn with half-smoked cigarettes. There was no shame or embarrassment involved in retrieving and collecting these, and many men carried empty tobacco tins for that specific purpose, crumbling open what they had gathered up and making new cigarettes with a packet of Rizla papers kept in the same tin.

My parents smoked Players Number Six, Embassy Regal or, on special occasions, Benson and Hedges, always considered a better quality cigarette because they were aimed at a better class of smoker, came in King Size and were packaged in a gold and black packet.

I was too late for cigarette cards – instead, I collected these from packets of loose tea and chewing gum – and, besides which, they always seemed to feature Famous Sportsmen of Yesteryear, in which I had no interest whatsoever.

I was thirteen when I started smoking, largely by stealing cigarettes in ones and twos from everyone around me.

My mother collected coupons, and once a year she ordered something from the cigarette manufacturers' catalogues. These so-called gifts were invariably disappointing. Comedians on the television joked that you could send away for an iron lung for only ten million coupons. The reality was closer to a set of six plastic egg cups for a thousand. It hardly mattered: people were smoking anyway, and so whatever was acquired with the coupons was, essentially, free. Just like the divi points totted up at the Co-op each visit, or the Green Shield stamps given out in impressive-looking sheets every time a few shillings' worth of petrol was put into the car.

When I was fifteen or sixteen, I gathered up hundreds of coupons, mostly from other people and cast-off packets, and sent off for a food-warmer designed to grace and complete any table setting and keep the food at a dinner party warm throughout the evening. It was something every hostess needed, apparently, and something she would not believe she had lived without. It was another world.

When it arrived, the food warmer consisted of a thin stainless steel box whose lid was perforated by a pattern of holes. Inside were two tea lights. Intended as a Christmas present for my mother, something to alleviate the daily domestic burdens of her life, it was the most disappointing thing I had ever seen. Upon receiving it, my mother was happy and grateful for the gift.

I doubt it had ever occurred to me to consider that not only did we never sit down as a family at a table for a meal, but that there was no table with its settings as such; or even that these so-called dinner parties never took place. Besides, we ate our dinners at midday and our last meal of the day, tea, between five and six. Nothing ever needed to be kept warm throughout the evening.

Afterwards, I became more adventurous in my choice of cigarettes, alighting briefly on menthol Consulates which were advertised as being like smoking and sucking a mint simultaneously, but which in reality was considerably less than either. Ten Consulates and everything about the world was both queasy and sickly sweet.

Health and smoking were never true concerns. People might have talked about there being some connection between smoking and lung cancer, but it was never a serious consideration, and anyone who both smoked and gasped for air was considered merely unlucky. Men worked down mines, or in dirty, smoke-filled factories. Some men said that smoking actually *cleared* their lungs. My mother referred to it as her only pleasure. She smoked fewer than my father, and often the smoke was coming down her nose while she was still sucking it in at her lips.

Experienced smokers knew when to tap off dead ash and when to leave the fading glow alone; others flicked too frequently, exposing an excess of still-burning tobacco to the air and wearing their cigarettes down without getting the full benefit. Old men sat in pubs concentrating on their games of cribbage, the whole length of their forgotten cigarettes turned to ash. Everyone dropped ash on to their sleeves or trouser legs and then brushed this to nothing.

It was always my ambition to blow smoke rings, something I never mastered. Accomplished smokers – men and women – showed off, blowing a succession of rings decreasing in circumference which passed outward through each other before dissolving into the air. Men held pint glasses and cigarettes in the same hand and drank and smoked in single gestures. It was forever a world worthy of my childish envy, a true rite of passage into the life beyond that childhood.

6

O NCE a year a man would turn up at our back door with a doctor's bag containing a ledger and wearing a mackintosh coat and a bowler hat. He was an agent for the land-holding company to which the owners and renters of the houses in our terrace still paid a ground rent almost a century after the small houses were built. I remember the sum as a guinea, making this already archaic transaction seem even more so.

The date was marked on a calendar and the agent solemnly awaited, the exact money always to hand. The man came into the house, sat at the fire, took the money, dropped it into his bag, usually without counting it, took out his heavy, solidly bound ledger, found our name and address, wrote in it, and then handed the book to my mother to countersign, which she did carefully and precisely, her signature never changing over the decades.

The transaction completed, the agent put on his hat, thanked everyone present, perhaps made some remark about our recent improvements to the house, and then left, crossing our yard to the neighbouring one, two paces away. Every house on the street paid this ancient due, as also, I imagined, did every other house on every other street around us. We were connected to a kind of history by the sum and the ritual of this transaction – a handful of coins endlessly and unavoidably extracted because of some greedy and far-sighted sub-clause on a hundred-year-old document.

On a more frequent, quarterly, basis, the gas man arrived to empty our grey metal meter of its shillings and sixpences, to make a note of the gas used, compare this to previous readings and then to reset the meter and reattach his clipped aluminium seal to the side of the box. He would also make a cursory check of the gas supply's ancient lead pipes and valves. The supply of gas was stopped and started by turning a tap set into a bulge in one of these pipes identical to the tap which controlled our water supply.

Once the meter was emptied out, the money was spread on a table and then swiftly and impressively assembled into dozens of short silver columns, each an exact and identical height. And following this, a percentage of this coinage was slid, croupier-like, back to my mother to be used again. The remaining columns were then scooped into another heavy satchel to be taken away and poured into the gas company's coffers. Those coins left behind were returned to stand on top of the meter in the cellar, ready to be fed back into the machine. It was often the only true credit we possessed, and the small piles were frequently borrowed or diverted according to other, more pressing needs.

There was no such elaborate or rewarding process for the electricity we used; instead, the meter was read and a bill duly arrived and my mother counted out the exact money demanded and took this to the Electricity Board's office and showroom in the city centre – just as she took the monthly mortgage payments to the Building Society office and, later, my school uniform payments to the city centre Co-op. In each instance, the accompanying paying-in book would be checked, stamped and countersigned, keeping debt at bay and a family afloat on the ebb and flow of credit and debit which endlessly washed over it.

The Ringtons Tea man came to the door with his wicker basket of strange teas. Onion men came all the way from France selling strings of onions to kind housewives. Sikhs in dramatic turbans showed up with their giant, impressively packed suitcases of cleaning products, capitalizing on the imperative to cleanliness which existed in most of those smoke-filled homes. These men always seemed simultaneously exhausted, cheerful and courteous, and sold as much by flattery as from genuine need. When children appeared alongside their mothers at the door there were precious miniature tins of polish and wax to be handed out as inducements. Besides, what home didn't always need another soft, unsoiled yellow duster or a genuine chamois – chammy – leather for all those dirty windows?

Once a year gypsies turned up selling lucky charms and pieces of desiccated heather. They were stout, head-scarved women with dark, weather-beaten faces. They often carried babies or had small children holding on to their floor-length skirts. They begged cups of water because another of those ancient laws said they could – that it wasn't really begging, that the householder had this unavoidable obligation to them. My mother gave them cups of tea, spoke to them, admired their babies, bought the cheapest of their charms and then locked the door and washed the cups when they'd gone. She stood at the front window watching them make their way further along the street.

People said the gypsy women had second sight, and my mother believed this. People said *she* had something similar, she insisted. Some of our neighbours, she told us, would see the women coming and then turn off their lights and hide from them. But not her. A gypsy curse on your house and your family was the last thing she needed. It was no joke. Things were bad enough as they stood without *that*. My father mocked her and complained at what little money she'd wasted on the lucky heather. Sometimes she bought lavender sewn into muslin bags and she gave us these to rub between our palms and sniff at, afterwards putting them in drawers to keep our clothes smelling nice. Why tempt fate? she asked my father. She could believe what she wanted, he told her, it was a free world.

7

WE left Ecclesfield when I was six, following the birth of my brother. My sister was three at the time. The house we came to added half a room on each floor to the usual two-up, two-down, in this case a narrow kitchen and a small bedroom into which a single bed for my sister barely fitted. A passageway led from the street to a divided rear yard. This passage was shared with a single neighbour, and our kitchen windows faced each other. Above the passageway to the rear of the house was a bathroom which contained our first hot water tap, bath and indoor toilet.

At the front of the house there was a garden a little wider than the pavement beyond, separating the front room window – a narrow but coveted bay – from the street with an unruly privet hedge and a laurel bush.

At the rear, down a few concrete steps and beyond the outside toilet and bin, was a garden comprising a twenty-foot-long lawn of patchy grass and moss surrounded by flower beds, in which my mother repeatedly sowed a variety of seeds with varying degrees of success. The grass was laboriously cut with a hand-pushed mower whose blades seemed forever blunt, and which mostly flattened rather than cut the grass. The only lasting flowers I remember are the vividly pink, red and orange lupins which grew against a sheltering wall.

The move from near-rural Ecclesfield into the city proper was undertaken to provide the extra space needed for our growing family. I shared a double bed with my brother for the next six years, followed by bunk beds until I was eighteen.

Soon after the flit, my father was dramatically taken into the nearby hospital in the middle of the night to have his ruptured appendix removed. At the same time, my mother's father, the only grandfather I had ever known, died of a heart attack in his late fifties. It was a great and unexpected loss to my mother, from which she struggled afterwards to recover.

To my young eyes and sensibilities, my widowed grandmother – my Nan – seemed hardly affected by the death, though of course she must have been. In all likelihood, Jack and Nellie would never have known anyone else on such close, dependent or intimate terms. That is not to say they didn't lead the largely separate lives of most older men and women at that time, but that they were inseparably bound by a history and a familiarity which, though outwardly invisible and unspoken – and often loudly and jokingly denied – was a sustaining strength, guide and comfort to them.

I remember nothing of the funeral or of grieving; small children were seldom a part of such things. All I knew for certain was that shortly after her husband's sudden and unexpected death, my Nan was forced to leave the immaculately kept and furnished council house she and Jack had shared, and was afterwards allocated a one-bedroom flat on the seventh floor of a tower block on the far side of the city.

She was later moved back into a house the same size and age as her original home, followed yet later by a maisonette with a warden, and which, like the earlier tower block with its fitted kitchen, unaffordable under-floor heating and lift access, seemed a leap into the modern world when compared to the crowded terrace into which my parents and their growing family had recently moved.

My Nan might have complained at these upsets and upheavals, but she accepted that, as a council tenant, the true choice was never truly hers to make, and that whatever complaints she might have had, the City Council was forever working as a benevolent force on her behalf.

Two small children, a new baby, a suddenly ill husband and then the equally unexpected death of her father – the months of all these other upheavals cannot have been easy for my mother. On top of which, she would soon be forced to resume working full time to supplement the housekeeping pot my father did little to maintain.

Regarding my father, it seemed to me throughout my childhood that we lived as two separate families – one which consisted of my mother and her three young children, and another into which my father's unwelcome and threatening presence constantly intruded. Everyone behaved differently when he was present; everyone was quieter, more guarded, and careful with their behaviour and what they said to each other. He found an argument in most things, a grievance to air, and other people's happiness and every small pleasure or achievement was forever negated by his own seemingly inexhaustible need to humiliate, to belittle, to control and to punish.

The house on Idsworth Road showed me acutely what we had left behind in Ecclesfield, what small freedoms I had lost. I went to a new and much larger school. I made new friends.

My younger sister and brother became the focus of my mother's attention and energy.

In every photo of our growing family following our move into the city, my mother changed from being the glamorous teenager she had once been upon falling pregnant for the first time into the overweight working housewife and mother of our overlapping childhood years. What did people expect? she would say. That was what having children did to women. It ruined their figures and then it took away their lives, their dreams, their hopes and their prospects. It was something else to factor into my father's continued frustration and unhappiness with family life. His own existence – at work and in the evenings and at weekends – hardly varied, and only my mother was truly forced to understand and then to respond to the demands of that changing life. Her good looks and her obvious appeal were quickly gone. Between the ages of nineteen and twenty-six she went – or so it seems in all those photos – from being a girl to a middle-aged woman.

8

T HE road was a hill, rising steeply from its base at the Page Hall junction, levelling out briefly halfway up, and then turning and rising again toward the Barnsley Road, beyond which lay the grounds of the Northern General Hospital. Our new home lay midway along the level part of the street, meaning that everything else was either up or down from us. Down, at the bottom corner, stood a small shop, and opposite this, on the steepest part of the hill, stood an old ballroom converted into a bingo hall.

Above our home, six doors away, stood a working men's club, by far the largest building in the neighbourhood, which held a thousand men, but with parking space for no more than thirty or forty cars. Beyond the club stood a more substantial house, and then, as the road rose to its summit, the stepped terrace resumed.

Across from our home, where the level land and opposite terrace ended, stood six inter-war semi-detached houses. These dwellings were always considered the road's best housing, and two of these possessed a short concrete driveway where the owners could park their cars.

Sheffield was a city of hills, and just as the road sloped from top to bottom, so it also crossed a hillside laterally, with the upper parallel street, Horndean Road, looking down on our terrace. A lower road lay beneath a sheer drop of twenty feet at the bottom of our small back garden.

In places, the land was too steep to build on, and small, overgrown patches filled with willowherb, elder and brambles sat amid the houses.

The pavements were tarmacked and narrow, and wherever a car was parked, the road was reduced to a single lane. In heavy rain, the water from the upper slope flowed the full length of the road and pooled at the bottom.

Page Hall was a collection of shops and gardenless terraces where doors opened directly on to the street. At the top of the road, running alongside the hospital grounds – to all intents a large woodland – the houses were larger and either detached or semi-detached with ornate porches and embellished lintels and gable ends. Steep paths climbed steep gardens to the front doors thirty feet above the road.

On a winter's morning, it was possible to walk down the street into a pall of smoke gathering in the frozen air from the hundreds of coal fires being coaxed into life. This was supplemented by the exhaust smoke from the cars, laboriously started and then left to warm up before journeys were begun.

The car parks at either side of the working men's club were spread with furnace waste, delivered once a year from a steel mill and dumped in warm, dusty mounds. Abrupt spaces between houses revealed where collapse or twenty-year-old bomb damage had yet to be repaired. All over the city, giant baulks of timber still buttressed exposed walls awaiting attention.

Both the major roads which bounded our street ran into the city centre, and both, in the opposite direction, returned via the giant housing estate to Ecclesfield and to the country-side beyond.

When I was older and owned a bike, half an hour's exhausting pedalling would return me to where I once lived. Inexplicably, then, it was important for me to know exactly where we now lay along those two routes, and as the city centre was rebuilt in the sixties and seventies, the two roads came to represent both a way forward and a way back for me.

The corner shop at the bottom of the hill was owned by the parents of my friend John, who lived above the shop in a room filled with the usual furniture and clutter, but which was supplemented by mounds of boxes and cases of foodstuffs and catering packs of cleaning products, giant tins and shrink-wrapped cartons – everything, in fact, that was on sale downstairs. A back yard to the shop was piled high with wooden crates and empty bottles. John's parents would take it in turns to attend to the shop and were frequently called back and forth, up and down their narrow staircase. They sold cheese and bacon and ham in single slices, and sweets and chocolates in penny amounts from an array of jars.

The shop was open fourteen hours a day, seven days a week. The solitary slices of ham were carefully wrapped in greaseproof paper and then folded into a brown paper bag, which Mr or Mrs Cave would then seal along its open edge with a deft, spinning and twisting motion. Cigarettes were sold to known children to take up the hill to their parents, and a slate was kept for regular customers. There was no shame in being put on the shop's slate. It meant that you were both valued and trusted; elsewhere, asking for credit would suggest only profligacy and fecklessness.

We visited the shop four or five times a day for our essentials, the downward journey always easier than the return.

Mrs Wilson lived in the last house before the club. She was one of the street's oldest and most impoverished residents, living in a decrepit and unsanitary house which you could smell as you passed it by. Mrs Wilson smelled the same, added to which was always the yeasty smell of bottled stout. She arrived at our back door on a weekly basis, first to pay off the few shillings she had borrowed the week before, and then to ask for a further loan of that same amount plus a little extra to see her through until her pension was paid to her in a few days' time.

As far as anyone knew, the old woman was entirely alone in the world. My mother always gave her the money out of her own purse. Mrs Wilson would pay my mother compliments on our home, on its neatness and comforts, on the smell of the food my mother was cooking, on the way her three beautiful, well-behaved and well-turned-out children were looking.

Sometimes, the old woman would ask for shilling coins to feed the gas meter, explaining perhaps that the meter had run out two days previously, but that she hadn't wanted to come and make a nuisance of herself any sooner than her usual, appointed hour. Mrs Wilson clasped my mother's hands, the money already in her own, and told her what a kind woman she was. When she'd gone, it was often necessary to spray air freshener where she'd stood. Each week, for years on end, this common drama of small courtesies and obligations was repeated at our door in exactly the same way.

My mother, Mrs Wilson always insisted, would go straight to Heaven when the time came. As would the rest of us simply by being related to her.

Sometimes, when I was playing in the club yard, I would climb a wall and look down into the old woman's house. Its windows were covered in dirt, the paint long gone, the wood-work rotting, the curtains unwashed and the nets yellow and disintegrating with age. There was the same small garden we possessed, but this one was high with nettles and dock, and strewn with empty brown bottles.

On one occasion, Mrs Wilson turned up at our door and asked my mother to read a letter she'd received. It was from Social Services, my mother explained to her, always something to be feared and avoided in that world. For all any of us knew, Mrs Wilson had lived in that same house all her life – she must have been at least seventy, a great age then – and none of us ever discovered anything about any family she might once have had. Upon being told who had sent her the letter, Mrs Wilson thanked my mother, promptly took it from her and folded it carefully back into its envelope. It was all she needed to know, she said. Concerned, and uncertain what to say next, my mother asked Mrs Wilson if she needed to borrow any money, and the old woman, suddenly preoccupied, said she didn't. She surprised even herself by this refusal, and then laughed and told my mother that she'd see her the following day at the usual time for the loan.

9

My father served his two years as a National Service conscript immediately before I was born. He had photographs of himself in the Army in Egypt, guarding the Canal, lounging in hammocks with his squaddie mates – his muckers – wearing boots and shorts and naked from the waist up. He was slim, wiry, wavy-haired and heavily tanned.

Along with his own upbringing, those two years in the Army informed the rest of his life and how he behaved as both a husband and a father – the two things being thrust upon him almost simultaneously upon his discharge from the Army. He picked up a few words of Arabic and whenever he wanted any of us to hurry he shouted *imshi imshi* at us, which, considering the words' exotic undertones, took some of the edge off his commands. Money was frequently referred to as baksheesh. His older brother had served those two years before him; his younger one would soon follow.

When we moved to Idsworth Road, the bedroom I shared with my young brother had a small closet, and my father's old kitbag was stored in this, packed tight with pieces of coarse clothing, folding mess tins and topped by a metal helmet. He kept the bag, he explained, because all National Servicemen were afterwards held in reserve, waiting to be called upon when a new emergency arose. The kitbag stood as a constant reminder to me of the happier and more fulfilled life my father had once lived before his premature marriage and the intrusion of his children. He went from school into labouring work into the Army into marriage with an already pregnant girl into father-hood. Everything about my father's young life was unavoidably determined by whatever had immediately preceded it.

He spoke fondly of Egypt – of the natives forever plotting to get one over on him and his oppos, of the stunts he pulled, bargaining down the cost of everything, reselling mucky post-cards of Arab women – and worse – who didn't care what they did to make money; of selling used tea leaves to the Arabs as tobacco, and then watching as the men rolled and happily smoked the leaves. Unbelievable.

Those same untrustworthy, devious, thieving Arabs lived at the bottom of our street. But not to worry – he had their measure.

Where did you do *your* bit? See any action? Active Service – same thing. Suez was practically a war.

My mother waited for him at home. I never saw any letters or postcards they may have exchanged. On Sunday mornings, my mother listened to *Armed Forces Family Favourites* on the wireless, messages and dedications between servicemen – Germany, Cyprus, Hong Kong – and their families at home. BFPO. Bill sends his love to Mam and Dad and says to Enid that it won't be long now until he's home. They were always the same songs about those homes and homesickness and home-coming; songs about longing and waiting and loving. Perhaps his absence did make my young mother's heart grow fonder, and perhaps that fondness led to her pregnancy, and the birth of that child – me – to everything that followed.

Later, on holidays or other rare excursions, my father would meet men like himself and they would discuss their shared pasts as conscripts in the Army. These men had their own similar photographs, tattoos and cigarette lighters. They might curse at the years lost to them as they had served their National Service – done their bit for Queen and Country – but it was at the same time a source of great pride to these men, an achievement of sorts in lives which afterwards appeared to contain few others.

Whenever I complained about hard work – and invariably after being told that I hadn't got the first idea what hard work was – I was told that digging holes in the desert sand was hard work, that putting up tents in the sand was hard work, that emptying out latrines was hard work, that marching and running in the desert sun was hard work. And when my mother complained about rare hot days, she was told that she didn't know what heat was. Summer in the desert, patrolling the Suez Canal – *that* was heat. Perhaps, without us, he would have signed on for longer and then become a proper soldier; perhaps everything conspired against him to prevent that from happening.

We watched black and white war films set in North Africa – Montgomery's Eighth Army, Rommel's Afrika Korps – and he pointed out to us all the details the film makers had got wrong. That wasn't even a proper salute. Nobody would be allowed to wear their belt or beret or even their long socks like that. If you were going to shoot over that distance, alter your sights first. They'd probably filmed the whole thing on Blackpool bloody beach, so *obviously* it didn't look real. In my young mind I conflated his National Service with the war and imagined him to have been a part of it. How, otherwise, was he able to point out all these mistakes with such authority?

Later, when I understood more, and through my obsession with Airfix models, Commando comics, and, consequently, the war itself, his remarks and criticisms became something for me to silently mock in my growing understanding of the man's endless need to be considered right and at the centre of things. *I* was the one who was able to identify planes, tanks, half-tracks, artillery pieces; *I* was the one who knew about the individual battles, who did what, where and when in the various campaigns, not him.

On the rare occasions I was brave enough to point out something I knew, or rarer still, correct something he'd just said, I was told that *I*'d be in a position to tell *him* what was what when I'd actually been in the desert with a rifle in my hands and with someone shooting at me. *Had* someone shot at him? Not the point, not the point. I was too bloody clever by half, that was my problem. But that's all I was – all books and lessons in my new school and no real experience of Life itself. I needed to learn to keep *it* shut. It was an easy enough lesson to learn. And I was supposed to be the clever one. And so we all kept our mouths shut and left him as the expert at our centre. Eventually, and as far as it was possible in that small house, we all simply avoided him.

The school of hard knocks, he called it. But they were the only lessons worth learning. Shout the loudest and win the argument. And when shouting didn't work, then there was always the threat of violence, followed by violence itself. He hoped we understood all this, and that we also understood that it was for our own good, that everything could have been worse, much worse. Everything he inflicted upon us served its purpose, and everything we learned like this was a valuable lesson. It had always been like that, always would be. And the sooner we understood this, the better it would be all round.

It was what made a man a good soldier. Obedience. Knowing exactly where he stood. Knowing just how far to push things, how far to go. The Yanks could keep their Hollywood actors; the men who mattered to him – and later to me – were those men – Richard Todd, Sam Kydd, Kenneth More – flying doomed bombers on vital raids, digging themselves out of prison camps, sitting mortally wounded beside a machine gun in that blazing desert waiting for the arrival of the Germans – or in a jungle somewhere waiting for the Japs, who were even worse – buying time for their comrades to get away, wiping the sweat from their brows, fighting off their wound-induced delirium and wearing their properly blancoed belts and carefully adjusting their gun sights as per regulation.

10

FOLLOWING our move from Ecclesfield, I attended Hucklow Road Infant and then Junior School. It was the same building divided in half, and the transition from one part to the other passed me by. It was a longer journey to the school than in Ecclesfield, where no location was far from anywhere else, and a journey the hundreds of children took wholly on foot, and mostly alone or holding the hands of older brothers and sisters in converging tributaries toward the school gates.

In the Junior School we sat at larger, shared desks, and a greater sense of routine was imposed upon us. Thanks to my mother, I could already read well, write well and had a basic grasp of fundamental mathematics. I started to learn the countries of the world, capital cities, longest rivers, highest mountains; I learned where forests, ice caps and deserts lay; I learned the kings and queens of England, the succession of Ages from the Stone Age through to the present. The greater order and pattern in all things was revealed to me. There was no need to consider my own or even my family's place in those given orders and patterns; things just *were*.

On the classroom walls there was a map of Sheffield, a map of the British Isles, a map of the world, a map of the rocks buried beneath me and a map of the planets, stars and moons above me. There were pictures of men dressed in furs living in caves; there was a queen with a fleet of ships battling a foreign Armada; there were castles and palaces, factories and farms.

Everything I believed I would ever need to know about the animals, birds, butterflies and fishes of the world I learned initially from the cards I collected from the packets of loose tea my mother bought daily. I learned to read using simple picture books that taught me more than I immediately understood. I knew what a noun was, a verb, an adjective and an adverb. I knew what ten per cent of eighty plus fifty per cent of sixty equalled. I could work out what everything cost in a shop and then check the change I received.

It was still a small, restricted world, but one that was slowly opening up and spreading perceptibly outward as I grew.

At Hucklow Road, school dinners were served in a canteen, and for the first time in my life I was given a hot meal which included a pudding in the middle of the day. Everything was served from wide metal trays and pans, and we carried our plates and cutlery and plastic beakers on another tray to our shared tables. I would relate to my mother in great detail everything I had eaten during the day; there was nothing I didn't enjoy. Every call for seconds and I was at the front of the queue.

The day was governed and measured by a hand-rung bell and we competed for the privilege and pleasure of ringing this at the nod of a teacher. We were given small bottles of milk each morning, and occasionally an apple or an orange.

Every afternoon, just as in Ecclesfield, the pig man came to collect the food waste. We were allowed to watch him through the window pushing his giant, wheeled bin to his stinking, fly-swarmed, food-encrusted lorry. He took away a full bin and left an empty one. It all made perfect sense to me.

A few years into my time at Hucklow Road, a sign was put up announcing the creation of a Television Room. A room with a television in it. A television that would be switched on during the daytime to show programmes made especially for schoolchildren. Curtains were drawn and lights switched off. For those of us who knew what a cinema was, we might almost have been there. Sheep farmers in Australia, beavers building dams and bears fishing for salmon in Alaska, tall skinny black men herding even skinnier cattle and goats across one of those deserts so familiar to my father: the world was at our fingertips and on our doorstep. I watched other black men loading boats with the oranges and bananas we ate as treats. I watched men blackened with coal digging it out from far underground lying on their backs; men ploughing vast fields of wheat; men flying the same jet aeroplanes which occasionally crossed the sky high above us, and which we all stopped to watch until they were invisible at the end of their long and perfectly straight white strings.

The ever present Nature Table, to which we were all encouraged to contribute, consisted of shells and rocks, leaves, feathers, small bones and skulls, acorns, fir cones and anything else to which the word Nature might, however loosely, be applied. Children brought in chrysalids and the dead birds or mice they had found. Birds' eggs were added, the discarded claws of cats, the powdery ball of a wasps' nest, a bird's nest, a jar of tadpoles, the desiccated corpse of a frog. In autumn, leaves were piled on the table, alongside acorns, chestnuts, haws and hips.

Occasionally, a sheep's skull or the horn of a sheep or cow was added to the exhibition. Yellow teeth were displayed.

Wasps and bees were trapped in jars, displayed for a day and then released, because that was the only fair thing to do. At all other times, a wasp was fair game and we trapped and killed them wherever we encountered them. Ants and beetles were gathered up in snuff and tobacco tins and displayed. These, too, were ceremoniously released. The skull of a bird or a mouse was a real treasure. Children returned from their sea-side holidays with shells and pebbles, and miniature beaches were constructed, to which were added the discarded legs and claws of crabs.

I started to collect brightly coloured, artificial – allegedly stuffed – birds, made of a kind of compacted cotton wool, with wire legs and claws, bead eyes and real feathers at the tips of their wings; and though these looked more tropical than native, they too were generously admitted to the Nature Table. The wire of the birds' claws meant that they could be attached to a branch and thus be made to appear even more lifelike.

A boy brought in a record of birdsong and a man's voice telling us the names of all the birds we were hearing. We were encouraged to listen for actual words and phrases in the songs, as though the birds might be attempting to communicate with us and thus repay our efforts in listening to them.

Another boy brought in a record of train noises and we sat cross-legged and swivelled our heads in unison as the hissing, clanking locomotives sped back and forth between the two speakers.

Hucklow Road School became half of my small world. I knew where all those other countries and oceans lay in rela-tion to my own home, my own street, and the streets between that home and Hucklow Road. I knew how people lived there, what occupations they carried out. I knew the names and habits of all the animals and birds, butterflies and fishes with which they were surrounded, just as I knew the names and habits of those which surrounded me. I could even recognize the call of some of those birds. They were all the complementary and memorable parts of a slowly expanding young life which fitted perfectly together, and which, as intended, drew that small, hungry and often fearful child beyond the boundaries and restrictions of his own existence.

11

DIRECTLY outside my grandmother's council house back door was a blackcurrant bush, nurtured, tended and cropped by my grandfather. It's faintly urine-like smell permeated the summer air. The bulk of their garden beyond a brick outhouse was an allotment upon which my grandfather grew vegetables and other hardy fruits. An actual allotment nearby was where he cultivated show-quality chrysanthemums – solitary giant heads on tall, supported stalks, cosseted and carefully trimmed into prize-winning blooms. My grandmother called them Grave Flowers and refused to have them in the house.

The old man – in his late forties when I was born – seemed both a constant affront and a challenge to my grandmother. He was a comfortable and slovenly dresser – collarless shirts, voluminous trousers, broad belts, white vests, hanging braces; he smoked heavily and non-stop. His hands were always dirty from his gardening, his boots forever threatening to traipse muck, leaves and worse into my grandmother's immaculate home.

My grandmother made jam from the blackcurrants, perhaps appreciating the availability of unlimited sugar after so long without. Raspberries were grown, apples, pears, plums and gooseberries. In a vegetable plot my grandfather produced potatoes, cabbages, carrots, marrows and onions, all a great pleasure and achievement to him as a wartime father of two young girls.

Everything my grandfather wore smelled of his life outdoors and of his tobacco. He wheeled barrow loads of manure to his plot from nearby smallholdings. There were frequently horses in the streets and he kept a shovel and a sack for when the animals appeared and dropped their dung in hard balls along the tarmac. He kept a compost heap and held my small hands to its warm and steaming surface. Even in the coldest of winter days the heap generated considerable heat.

He presented all his foodstuffs to my grandmother, who would clearly have preferred shop-bought. The war was over; none of this was *necessary* any longer; they could afford to buy everything now in the shops.

At the end of each day together, he and I stood over the burgeoning marrows and cucumbers and pissed on the straw which supported them. He told me this was good for the vegetables, that they needed as much piss as they could get. He often stood with a cigarette dangling from his mouth, his braces at his thighs. It was our secret, he told me. Let the others eat all they wanted, but not us. He winked at me when my grandmother offered the tinned salmon and cucumber sandwiches round every Sunday tea time.

My grandfather taught me how to catch butterflies by loosely throwing a jacket over them where they sat on a plant and then sliding my hand up an empty sleeve to feel them fluttering inside. He gave me sips of dark stout from the bottles he secreted away from the house. He taught me gentle swear words and then paid me to utter them in the company of my amused father and disapproving mother and grandmother.

Most Sundays while we lived close, we would go to their house for our tea. The sandwiches of Sunday tea, at my grandparents' house and later our own, were always followed by tinned fruit cocktail, evaporated milk and bread and butter. Throughout my childhood and teens, bread and margarine was what filled us up. If we ever complained of hunger, then extra slices were produced and added to the mound at the centre of every table. Actual butter was always presented in butter dishes, usually yellow or cream-coloured and often featuring a cow to emphasize further that it was real butter and not some cheaper substitute. Before we owned a fridge, the coolest part of every house – pantry or cellar head – was sought out for keeping dairy produce fresh.

Accompanying all these special meals was a succession of pots of tea. On Sunday, the special tea service was taken out from my grandmother's display cabinet. Cups and saucers, spoons alongside, even a bowl for sugar and a small jug for milk. But the highlight of the meal was the ceremoniously opened tin of salmon. The fish with their jutting jaws featured prominently on the labels and the soft meat inside was carefully spread over enough bread to feed five or six people. The first salmon most people had seen had been delivered as part of the American lend-lease food parcels which had arrived during the war, and everything about the small cans held meaning and pleasure which lasted for long afterwards. Some people, it was laughingly said, were too posh for the salmon and so ate only cucumber sandwiches, forever the mysterious height of refinement.

Later, when I started junior school, poorer children arrived with apple or onion sandwiches for their dinner. Some ate crisp sandwiches and some pretended to enjoy sandwiches of dry bread and tomato sauce.

My grandfather would eat his bowl of fruit salad and then make a point of licking out the creamy residue of his bowl. Likewise, he would always pour the tea from his cup into his saucer and then drink it from this, exaggerating his slurps for comic effect and insisting to my grandmother that he needed to cool the liquid down. The old man's complete lack of table manners – something drilled into the rest of us – would be confirmed by his belching and by his use of the best china saucers as ashtrays. The man was a comic turn and everything he did and said made me laugh, often for no other reason than that I loved him and he always wanted me on his side. I sensed that even though his wife and daughter pretended to be offended by his behaviour, they too were amused by him and that both, in their own way, indulged and encouraged him.

The burden of her husband's presence was forever pointed out by my grandmother. It made her own achievement in keeping their home immaculate and well provisioned all the greater. It was a great compliment to the cook, a belch, my grandfather always announced. In France it was the done thing. We weren't in France, one of the women would tell him. Thank God for that, he would say.

After eating, there might even be a bottle of that dark stout, drunk alongside the tea, and the women would sip at glasses of sherry. Cigarette smoke would fill the room, and the hour after the meal – the end of the weekend, half a day away from the start of another long working week – was a time of great contentment. Children would be sent out to play, and any babies bedded down on the settee. It always seemed to me that something of great importance had been achieved in those meals, a small success won, a kind of survival almost.

When my grandfather died, the teas continued for a time but were never the same. For my grandmother, keeping the house clean without his obvious intrusions into her realm seemed suddenly less of an achievement or pleasure. Now a widow, she was moved soon afterwards into her tower block and the Sunday teas ended completely.

The family story told most often and consistently about my grandfather was that during the war, too old and unfit to be called up for active service, he had served as an air-raid warden in Sheffield city centre. As part of these duties he had acted as a spotter for planes and fallen bombs, perched high on the roof of a department store. The story goes that, because he was a chain-smoker he was repeatedly warned about smoking on duty – 'presenting a light to the enemy' it was called, adding to the tale's seriousness and alleged veracity – but that he was unable to resist. As a consequence of this, he was suspended from his duties – perhaps even arrested – and this, according to my father, brought great shame on my mother's family. Showing a light, *signalling*, even, to the enemy – almost as though the young pilots and bomb-aimers high above him and returning night after night to the heavy industries of the South Yorkshire coalfields and the steel mills of the Don Valley might be looking out for the solitary flickering cigarette end of a frightened old man standing alone on the top of a high building, all around which the bombs were already falling.

To me, there was always something simultaneously ludicrous and admirable about the tale – that single, minuscule point of light amid square miles of conflagration, volcano-like fires and explosions – and something which perfectly encapsulated the man I knew and loved.

When we were alone together I would ask him about the war and he would make up stories to satisfy my lurid imagination, his hands turned to aeroplanes. He told me how everybody else in the family, my grandmother, mother and aunty included would be sitting in shelters or crouched under tables terrified, listening out for the distant bombs and counting the seconds between explosions.

After he died, my grandmother was reputed to have found bundles of money hidden all over their home and in my grandfather's outhouses and sheds: twenty pounds, fifty, a hundred, all wrapped in rubber bands and stuffed into pots and jars and tobacco tins. These were welcome discoveries now that her already small pension was halved and there was a funeral to pay for. Welcome, but not all that surprising to a generation of hoarders forever keen to prepare for the coming hard times ahead of them. Our cellar head at home was never without its supply of tinned salmon, fruit cocktail and evaporated milk for at least the next twenty years.

12

A T the bottom of the back garden our boundary wall, waist-high to us when we stood there, dropped to the lower garden of the terrace below. Standing at the wall, we overlooked the mirror image of our own home, yard and garden. And in the house immediately beneath us lived a man with a spine so badly deformed and curved that it bent him double and caused him to walk with his face at the level of his waist and looking at the ground. Predictably, and with the casual cruelty of children, we called him the Hunchback.

I doubt if the unfortunate man ventured often or far from his home. His only regular outing as far as I could see was when he left his back door each teatime – five-thirty or six – and then ran down the yard to his own outside toilet. When we saw him on this regular excursion we called down to him, mocking him and perhaps causing him to run faster in an attempt to hide himself from us. None of us could tell if he was twenty or seventy, so severe was his deformity, but knowing even this much about him would have made no difference to our behaviour.

If my mother caught us laughing at the man, or even if she heard of it afterwards, she punished us. The man lived with his own mother; he was somebody's son. We should feel sorry for him, pity him and spare a thought for the terrible life he was forced to live. There but for the grace of God… she told us. Besides, none of us knew how he had come to be so deformed. Perhaps the man had had a serious accident. An accident at work, perhaps. Perhaps he'd been a miner, a man in a foundry; perhaps he'd fallen from scaffolding. Or perhaps, worse, much worse: perhaps he'd been born like that and there was nothing the doctors could do for him. Whatever the cause of his deformity, the burden and misery of his existence was his and his poor mother's alone to bear.

And besides, my mother said, suppose no one had known in advance of how he would come into the world, no one had expected. Suppose his mother had been anticipating a normal, healthy baby. Imagine that. Perhaps, my mother added, he hadn't even been expected to live beyond being that tight clenched ball of a baby.

We could imagine very little of this, of course. We ought to know better, she told us. She hadn't brought us up to behave like that. We ourselves might have been born with deformities, so imagine that, too. It could just as easily have happened to any one of us.

We mimicked the man's scuttling run to the toilet. It was probably painful even to stand like that, let alone walk or be forced to run, my mother said. It was a terrible existence, and we were making it so much worse for the poor man. And it was only because she knew how it would add to the man's misery, my mother told us, that she wasn't insisting on us going to the house, knocking on the door and then apologizing to him and his mother in person. His despairing mother, she added, probably prayed to God every day of her life – anything to ease or to end her son's misery. It was all a joke to us, a joke, she said. Well, not everything was funny; not everything existed just to make us laugh or feel better about our own lot in life.

13

B EYOND my father's drinking companions, my parents had few friends. Neither of them invited or encouraged people to visit us at home because of the time he spent in the house without his wig on. We children were certainly warned against encouraging any of our own friends to come and call for us.

In this and many other ways, the distinction between family and all others was always precisely understood and carefully maintained. According to both my parents, family – however much you mistreated them and maligned them in private, and they you – counted for everything; no one else came even close. Blood was always thicker than water. There were rules and regulations governing families which were broken or ignored only at considerable risk and cost. By this simple reckoning, even the closest friend or workmate was nothing compared to the most distant, little-known, seldom-visited cousin. If you didn't have your family, then who else did you have? Having your health and good fortune was all well and good, but what good were your health and good fortune if you didn't have a family around you to share and rejoice in that good health and good fortune?

That said, my father argued with his brothers and sisters, and enmities repeatedly flared; conflicts and silences were maintained for months, years even. It was all a simple matter of people needing to learn where they stood. There was always a pecking order in that family, and my father always considered himself to be somewhere near the top of it.

And just as my father took great satisfaction in replicating his own childhood punishments and restrictions, so he took even greater pleasure in telling us while meting out these punishments how much more considerate, patient and lenient *he* was being with us when compared to how his own father had been with him. We all quickly came to understand this for the contrived and self-serving excuse it was.

It was occasionally possible to say something cruel or deprecating about a relative, but only depending on whether or not that relative was in or out of favour at the time. Brothers- and sisters-in-law, for instance, were frequently cast to the edges of the family circle. The men were never good enough for the three sisters; women never quite came up to the mark for the three brothers. Even my mother was occasionally compared to my father's sisters and found wanting. The husbands of the three girls were singled out for the closest scrutiny by my father, and the very least they could expect was disparagement and mockery. As ever, some targets were always easier and more worthy of being struck than others.

Tales spread quickly through the entire family on strong winds. Unsubstantiated yet elaborate stories were repeated for decades after their first airing.

Our neighbours, too, were commonly treated as an inconvenience by my father. Many of the passageway footsteps were false alarms and he leapt wigless from his seat in front of the television for no good reason. Those few people knocking at our own back door were kept there until we knew him to be safely upstairs, where he would either wait for the visitor to be turned away, or where he would put on his wig and come back down. Relatives would never turn up unannounced, so why should these others? His waiting presence, whether behind the stair door or upstairs sitting on the bed, staring past the polystyrene head into the mirror, was always keenly felt by those of us downstairs who knew exactly what was happening.

The only other people who ever came to our door were the men and their wives who my father met in his pubs, or the couples my mother and father encountered together on the few rare occasions she went out with him, usually to the working men's club along the street. A succession of so-called uncles and aunties came, were the be-all-and-end-all in my father's eyes, and then afterwards fell out with him and subsequently disappeared from our lives just as quickly as they had arrived.

The lives of these people always seemed more exciting to me than the lives of my parents, and while my father was able to pretend both to himself and to them that he lived exactly the same kind of life they did, my mother cannot have felt anything but cowed and wary of these encounters founded mostly on regular and heavy drinking together.

Men would appear and tell us how lucky we were, what a wonderful and generous man our father was. The tales he told, the jokes he recounted, the things he'd done, the places he'd seen, the drinks he'd bought. Sometimes, in the company of these others, my father would behave exactly like that wonderful man and give us money, the change from his pockets. These other men often followed his example and did the same. See? What a man.

Being children, and because we neither understood nor were shown how other people in other families behaved, we accepted these gifts and agreed with the flattering remarks of those other men. Perhaps my father went to their homes and behaved in precisely the same way toward their own children.

And then these people would disappear from our lives. There had been a row, a disagreement, a falling-out, words had been exchanged. People were never what they seemed, so good riddance to them. Good riddance to bad rubbish. You thought you knew who your friends were and then they did *that* to you.

Sometimes, my father flirted with the wives of these men, occasionally in front of my mother. And sometimes their husbands were sober enough to take offence at this. People got drunk and spoke their minds. The only problem with these sudden ruptures was that my father had then to consider where he went to do his drinking, on what nights and in which pubs he might now encounter these lost friends and new enemies.

It was often said that my father used the kind of language that even these other hard-working, hard-drinking men found offensive; especially when he used it in front of their wives. He was too forward, too full of himself, too swift to turn abusive. I imagine that after these fallings-out they all laughed at him because of his wig. All those other people might pretend not to notice, but once these so-called friends had turned against him, it was an obvious and justified point of mockery for them. And how could you ever re-establish a friendship with a man who had pointed out to you that you were wearing a wig and all this suggested about your character? Pointed out to you that you were wearing a wig and that everyone *knew* you were wearing a wig.

On one occasion, a whole Christmas was ruined when my father came home in a drunken rage on Christmas Eve after a works party and shouted at my mother that a woman in the garage had accidentally knocked the supposedly secure hairpiece from his head when she was dancing. He'd been the laughing stock, he said. The woman might have apologized, but by then it was too late. He spent the whole holiday in another of his angry sulks, and we knew to avoid him. We went through the usual – and normally pleasurable – routine of the holiday, but that was all. One of the few long-anticipated events of our year had been ruined and we were powerless to salvage anything of the occasion. We would all now have to wait another full year.

My father dreaded returning to work on the day after Boxing Day, but he did go and then came home each night and refused to say any more about what had happened.

On another occasion, one of his drinking companions came to the house and suggested that he should relax and that if he wanted to, he could… you know… The man nodded at my father's head. My father said that no, he didn't know what the man was getting at. You know… your… The man ran his fingers through his own hair. But still my father refused to understand him. Finally, sensing the mistake he had made, the man said, Okay, have it your own way, finished his drink, smoked another cigarette and then said he was leaving. My father went through to the front room to peer through the net curtains at the man driving away and then returned to us in another rage, asking us over and over who the man thought he was. Well, that was him finished. What a bastard. And in my father's own home, having accepted my father's hospitality, having spent months together in the same few boozers and clubs.

Turning to his silent, waiting children, my father said he hoped we'd been watching and that we'd learned a lesson about all these other people out there, that we now understood how quickly – and for absolutely no reason whatsoever – how quickly they were happy to turn on you.

My mother, in all likelihood, was relieved to see the back of yet another of these fair-weather companions, no longer forced to witness and acknowledge all those other lives being lived more fully and happily than her own, though which, in all likelihood, were probably little different.

14

THE Devlins lived across the street in an end-of-terrace house. They were devoutly Catholic Irish and their accents and harsh, spat-out language were largely unintelligible to us. They were thin, pale-skinned, dark- or red-haired, suspicious, foul-mouthed and quickly violent.

The father was regularly to be seen staggering like a comic drunk up the hill, frequently stopping to catch his breath, steady his balance, spit copiously at his feet and then loudly and incoherently berate any passer-by. He often stood at the kerb throwing up into the gutter. His wife came out of their house and threw buckets of cold water over his vomit – more, possibly, because, like all the women on the street, she took a proprietorial care in this extension of her domain, than out of any true sense of loyalty to her drunken, violent husband.

It was common knowledge that the man had a constant temper and that he was handy with his fists. He often stood like a boxer, warding off those passers-by as he waited to continue walking. It was also common knowledge that he beat his wife and children; their rows and crying could frequently be heard along the street. On occasion, Mrs Devlin would follow him as he set off on one of his drinking sprees, shouting and cursing at him, carrying a baby and with at least one other small child at her side. There were six children in total, four boys and two girls, and all of them to be feared and avoided whenever possible.

The Devlins set the lower level of the street as far as public behaviour and family life were concerned, and we all in one way or another judged ourselves against them and smugly appreciated their presence in our midst. However low anyone else might sink, we reasoned, they would never sink anywhere near as low as the Devlins had already sunk.

I only once went inside their dark, overcrowded house, and was surprised there by the large painting of Jesus which hung above the fireplace and loomed over the room. It looked to me, more accustomed to those plastic pebbles and golden sunbursts, like a picture that belonged in an art gallery. The robed, bearded man held out his hands, palms up, to the viewer below, and rays of vivid light shone outward in another sunburst from behind him. I laughed at seeing the picture and was immediately punched and told to shut my mouth. It was Our Lord, I was told admiringly, and everything that existed in this world and happened in life existed and happened because of Him and only because of Him. Even the youngest children repeatedly crossed their chests in front of the portrait. It was an uncomfortable home, with dark, ancient furniture and peeling linoleum, and forever thick with the smell of damp, carbolic and endlessly simmering pans.

Like my sister, brother and me, the Devlin children were left to their own devices during the daytime when there was no school. They patrolled the neighbourhood, stealing, bullying and fighting; an insult to any one of them – however unintentional or manufactured – was an insult to them all. The older boys came and went from neighbouring yards and gardens, knocking on doors and windows and demanding money and food.

Some of our neighbours, knowing the father, took pity on the children and handed out biscuits or slices of bread. None of this was appreciated by the Devlins; a solitary lapse in generosity and they were again instantly abusive and aggressive. Mrs Devlin stood outside houses and cursed people for their charity. My father said they were no better than animals; worse – gypsies. Which, being Irish and Catholic, was probably how they'd started out. Once again, it all made perfect sense to him.

When the drunken father fell and was unable to stand, the older boys were sent out to help him up from the pavement and guide him home. Anyone pausing to watch this was chased away by these vicious guardians. One of the Devlins' specialities – the girls included – was to spit at people. Even the slightest confrontation and they hawked up phlegm and spat in people's faces. Boys along the street who occasionally cornered one of the younger Devlins lived for days afterwards in fear of reprisals from the older ones.

Mr Devlin hit his own wife and children in view of the street and threatened any witnesses with the same.

My own constant fear of the Devlins was mixed with pity for them. My father was equally capriciously violent and bullying, and often the worse for wear, but at least everything *he* inflicted on his wife and children was kept private, in the home, afterwards deniable or glibly explained away. With the Devlins, the violence was all too obvious on their thin faces and limbs and there for all to see.

The Devlin girls were seen out of the house less frequently, and seldom unaccompanied by one of their older brothers. On the occasion of my only visit, the girls were on their hands and knees washing the floor, suspicious of me and uncomfortable in my unexpected presence.

From my bedroom window, I often saw the older boys climbing out of their own upstairs rooms and dropping first to the bay window and then to the street below, changes of clothing thrown down after them. The oldest two, Patrick and Danny, aged fifteen or sixteen, started to accompany their father on his nightly wanderings, and because this made them no longer children in my eyes, they lost some of their threat to me. At the first possible opportunity, the boys left the school they had hardly attended and found labouring jobs, following the path of their father. The younger boys took their place. Nothing ever prevented a seven- or eight-year-old Devlin from launching himself at a boy twice his age or size.

Frequently, whenever I or my brother or sister complained about something, we were told to stop moaning and then to consider how much worse things would be if we had Mr and Mrs Devlin for parents. But this was never an argument in my eyes, and only added to my contempt for the family. Every time one of them appeared in the street and spotted me at my bedroom window I would duck down and pretend I wasn't there. None of this prevented the stone throwing, which the Devlins enjoyed as much as their spitting.

Truancy and Welfare Officers were regular visitors at the Devlin home, shouted away from the doorstep by Mrs Devlin. I was told by my mother that the children attended a Catholic school and she described this to me as being more of a church than a place of learning, and certainly nothing to compare to my own school.

On Sundays – Mr Devlin as sober as he ever appeared – the family marched to church in an orderly, largely silent, line. It was the only time I ever saw any external force govern to the slightest degree the behaviour of any member of the family. The services lasted all morning, and afterwards the family returned home without the father.

To my own father, the Devlins were Paddies and Micks, thick as the proverbial two short planks, shifty and untrustworthy and not worth the effort of arguing with. The only time he paid any real attention to the drunken father or roaming boys was when one of them went too close to his precious cars, knowing even then that it was safer to watch from behind net curtains than to go out and confront any of them directly.

Catholics, my father said, bred like rabbits, and the Devlins were living proof of that. The two girls would be knocked up before they knew it, and the house across the road would be forever filled with the vicious little bastards that passed as children. We should pride ourselves, he told us, that we weren't anything like them, and that we never would be. Micks – and he'd met enough of them during his Army days to know – were nice enough to you when it suited, but they'd lie through their teeth to you and then cheat or rob you the minute your back was turned.

The Devlins sometimes seemed more foreign to me than any of our West Indian or Pakistani neighbours, and for the whole of my time on that street, they remained the living embodiment of my father's every prejudice.

15

M Y father was rarely out in public, and certainly never in one of his bars, without wearing his jewellery. He favoured heavy, yellow gold. His shirt cuffs were always studded with cufflinks – gold and black enamel or gold and mother of pearl, something for him to stand and twist as he drank. And because he wore cufflinks, he also wore elasticated gold-plated sleeve holders, which he drew up his arms to his biceps and then released into place, tugging down his white shirt sleeves until they hung an exact distance beneath his jacket and thereby displayed the cufflinks to best effect.

He wore signet rings with either ebony or gold coin faces, heavy gold link bracelets and always either a thin gold chain or medallion around his neck.

In summer, the pale blond hairs of his chest caught in the links of his chains and he endlessly released these. When he later wore reading glasses, these too had gold side-pieces. His shoes were often buckled – sometimes in grey leather with elasticated sides and a heavy clasp looking two centuries out of date.

Other men admired what he wore, women too; they were meant to.

When self-winding watches became all the rage, he bought one of these and then showed us all how to rewind it with a few flicks of his wrist so that it ran for a week. Gold watch straps matched his armbands. Later, when folding stainless steel straps became fashionable, he owned one of these, too. Stainless steel was what Sheffield was famous for, and this connection – this loyalty, almost – persisted in my own mind for long afterwards as I bought my own first watches and cigarette lighters.

And along with his jewellery, my father possessed a switch-blade knife: a four-inch blade folded into a Perspex and gold handle featuring a bullfighter and a bull. The solitary blade was released by pressing a spring-loaded catch at the head of the handle. My father hid the knife in my parents' dressing table, but I found it and was fascinated by it, forever taking it from its hiding place and playing with it. When my father was at work I took it outside and threw it into the tarry telegraph poles outside our house.

The knife hinted at something dangerous, violent and excit-ing in my father's past, in the years between him leaving school and serving his National Service, but whatever that might have been remained unknown to me.

All this extravagance – I remember nothing of the jewellery my mother might have worn – was enhanced by his acquisition and display of all these pieces. Gold was gold, you couldn't go wrong. Gold was as good as money in the bank, better. Backstreet pawnbrokers had windows and cabinets full of the stuff. Gold marked a man out, made him a cut above. I daresay many other men kept their cuffs at the same exact, revealing lengths, but the only other times I remembered seeing those expanding-link gold armbands was on the arms of Mississippi riverboat gamblers during our Sunday afternoon black and white television westerns.

16

W HEN I was eight I was sent for the first time to Sunday School. Saint Cuthbert's: a sandstone-built, ornate and imposing Victorian church on the corner of Barnsley Road and Firvale, surrounded by a walled mound and a succession of smaller buildings and huts which served the church's various societies and associations. Like the chapels in Ecclesfield, the sand-coloured blocks, lintels, sills and door-frames of the church had long since been turned black by the industrial air of the city.

At Sunday School I was told about the Bible and we sang hymns. Scripture – all the stories of the Bible – formed a large part of that dusty hour or two. The vicar's wife was in charge and we were all sent to her in our Sunday best clothes. I had no idea of the true purpose of the institution; its whole meaning seemed encapsulated in its name. But whatever we achieved or learned there, we were all convinced that we were better children for it. Occasionally, we were rewarded with pop and cakes or sweets, and this above all else made the experience worth enduring. We chanted together and every correct answer earned its praise or small reward. It was a novel experience for me, and something else which appealed about the place. Where it counted or reaped some benefit for me, I developed my skills as a show-off, performing and shouting out answers to attract attention to myself that didn't end with me being told either to shut up or to show some manners, or worse. After all, nobody liked a show-off.

From Sunday School it was a natural progression to Saint Cuthbert's Cub Troop, a precursor to the Scouts. Saint Cuthbert's 114th. Even the title made our childish, militaristic blood flow faster and our young bodies stiffen.

We wore green caps and a green jumper. Our long green socks were held up with decorated, scarlet garters, of which we were inordinately proud. Round our necks we wore a twisted length of navy and white material held in place by a leather woggle, in which was embedded the symmetrical brass head of a wolf.

The double-ended neckerchief was the same size as one of my mother's headscarves. At the back of our heads, beneath our tight caps, a blue-edged triangle of the material was eased out into a flap and smoothed down over our jumpers.

Every Wednesday night began with a prayer, a pledge of allegiance to the Queen, a gathering of subscriptions, mostly in pennies, and a uniform inspection, where particular attention was paid to the neckerchief, woggle and cap, followed by our socks and garters. I felt inexplicably happy at the Cubs, standing to attention in the uncomfortable clothing.

There was a shop in the city centre devoted to the sale of the various outfits. A chart on the shop wall displayed the countless combinations of neckerchief, woggle, cap and garters adopted by the multitude of other troops around the city. The shop also sold second-hand uniform parts, and everyone I knew at Saint Cuthbert's came dressed in this cheaper clothing. As elsewhere in my life, where money always needed saving, there was no shame in this. We were growing, active boys and the shorts and jumpers were quickly worn through and damaged. Even the caps were second-hand. The only items we were encouraged to acquire brand new were the scarves and woggles. These, we were told, would remain precious mementoes for life.

As I was later also to be told at grammar school, I was to consider myself a different person when I was in uniform, especially when I was out in public – on my way to or from a meeting, for instance, attending a jamboree, or when I was required to attend some church ceremony or other. Any misbehaviour or slovenliness on my part would reflect badly on us all and invariably be reported back to the pack leader, Akela, a pale, gangling man with B.O. and an overactive Adam's apple. He was accompanied by his wife, who was double his size. He told us that whenever we were in uniform, then he was our father and she was our mother. The woman tended to our grazes and cut knees and elbows, when everything was liberally swabbed in TCP. It stung and it hurt and it was meant to.

We were taught the essentials of woodcraft – identifying trees and animals and birds. We were shown how to track and trap those animals and birds, how to forage for food, how to make water drinkable, how to build a bivouac, how to fasten every knot imaginable. We were taught how to light fires and then how to cook a simple meal using that fire. We made bread twists, creating dough from flour and water and then holding this on a stick over the flames to bake and scorch. We sat around these fires in the grounds behind the scout hut as though we were far out in an unmapped wilderness. We started learning the social duties of a cub which, along with our attendance at Sunday School, was turning us into better, more responsible, more capable people.

I unsuccessfully pestered my mother for a particular brand of shoe, the sole of which displayed the footprints of half a dozen wild animals, and the heel of which concealed a small compass. I was taught that I would never be lost or hungry or without shelter in the world, and that whatever wilderness did exist beyond the light of the campfire would hold no fear for a boy of the 114th Saint Cuthbert Cub Troop. It was an enduring fantasy and one greatly appreciated by us all.

17

My father and his two brothers followed near-identical paths into their adult lives. All left school in their mid-teens with no or few rudimentary qualifications. All did their National Service, and then, at twenty or thereabouts, all three of them left the Army, met someone, became engaged to be married, got married, quickly started their own families and found themselves labouring jobs to support all these sudden, uncertain and demanding commitments. By their early twenties, they were all family men with the rest of their lives already mapped out ahead of them.

Their own father had died aged thirty-eight and was absent from all these crucial early junctures of their young lives. They had all been boys during the war, and now found themselves as the heads of families in a city still a long way from having recovered from that war.

By their mid-twenties, all three men had graduated from hard labouring to working with heavy vehicles of some kind.

Ray and Tony, the eldest and youngest boys, started work as long-distance lorry drivers. In the days before motorways, or even dual carriageways and ringroads, this would frequently entail absences of two or three nights a week and the men sleeping in their cabs, eating at cafes catering solely for lorry drivers, and then returning home exhausted to make the most of the brief time with their wives and children.

My father worked for a lorry-recovery firm with a sideline in house removals. After this, he moved to a national chain of garages specializing in the recovery, repair and servicing of several better makes of car, including, much to my father's pride, Rolls-Royce. At some point, he became a store manager for one of these branches – the man responsible for keeping the storerooms filled with all the necessary parts and products for this service, repair and recovery work to take place.

He began calling himself Management and started going to work in a shirt and tie and a suit, the jacket of which was replaced upon his arrival at the garage with a long brown overcoat to protect his clothes from the greases and oils with which all men who worked with cars and lorries seemed to be permanently coated.

In addition to these smarter clothes, he took to carrying a slim briefcase of tan-coloured imitation leather which contained his flask, sandwiches and a folded newspaper. One of my mother's tasks upon his return from work each day was to retrieve this case and empty it. The next morning, she would replenish its contents. These never varied. In reality, the imitation leather was a kind of compressed cardboard, and this quickly revealed itself around its edges.

My father stayed at this work for most of his working life, and his daily timetable and weekly routines were rigidly adhered to. Later, a few years before his retirement, he returned to lorry driving, lighter haulage now, and over shorter distances, there and back in less than a day. He always took great satisfaction in discussing various routes with other drivers, telling them how to save time, money, tyre rubber and petrol by following his own recommendations. A conversation about the benefits or otherwise of a new road opening or a town bypass would last for at least half an hour.

Tony, the youngest brother, barely fourteen when his father died, drove for a firm of skip-providers and waste-removers, dropping off the empty containers and then retrieving them when they were full, and delivering these to one of many vast landfill sites along the industrial, northern edge of the city, where we all lived.

In large part, this was industrial refuse, including tankers full of toxic liquid waste, used oils or spent chemicals which were a by-product of the nearby steel mills and foundries. He wore protective clothing and heavy gauntlets and told stories of spraying oily sludge over the surface of the landfill sites to flush out their populations of rats. He said men waited for his arrival with air rifles and terriers to shoot and chase the fleeing vermin.

Ray had four children, my father three, Tony two. So, in addition to my father's own three sisters, we children acquired two further aunts. The women were a welcoming, ameliorating force in that family of men, where most of the annual socializing was almost always a wholly exclusive affair with few outsiders involved.

My father's three sisters were called Val, Gloria and Mary.

Val married Arnold, a bus conductor, and the pair of them raised their own family of two boys in the same house in the middle of the council estate in which her parents had lived, and in which she, aged twenty-one, had then helped to raise all the other, younger, suddenly orphaned children.

My first memory of being with Gloria and Mary – Mary always referred to as the baby of the family – was of sitting in my pram at some kind of garden fete, perhaps Ecclesfield's annual fair. I remember the pair of them at the pram's raised handle, talking to me and stopping to show me off to everyone who demanded to look. It was rough ground and the jolting ride added further to the excitement of being with the two girls like this. Gloria was twelve when I was born, Mary eleven.

The girls must have walked from their parentless home on the estate to where my young parents were living two miles away. Perhaps my mother had found work elsewhere – I doubt she was working full time then – or perhaps she was just happy to have some time to herself, overwhelmed by her own rapid and unexpected progress from being a teenage girl to a young wife and mother in an already demanding marriage.

Gloria later married Judd and had two daughters. Much later, Mary married David and had two boys.

This expanding family grew into a precise and predictable shape, largely governed and regulated by how things had always been done in the past.

Ray told his own stories connected to his work – of attaching a chain to the front axle of his lorry to kill the rabbits he encountered in their hundreds on the early morning roads he drove along, hitting these and then gathering them up to either sell or eat upon his return home. Rabbit featured almost weekly in our own meals, another not-so-distant echo of that wartime rationing and frugality, and every butcher in the city worth his salt still had them dangling limply in his window.

A further fond and lasting memory of my two young aunties is of their ability to whistle. Both girls were able to create the loudest, longest and purest whistle by the simple measure of touching the tips of their various fingers to the corners of their mouths. The fingers were placed, the top lip curled out and down to conceal the lower and then the slightest of blows given to produce the siren-like blast. Close to, the sound was genuinely painful, and it could be heard at a great distance through traffic and all other noise.

Afterwards, I only ever heard that same whistle used by television shepherds controlling their dogs over wide open spaces and long distances.

There was a solitary variation to this type of whistle, one which involved one of the longer fingers, fore or index, being tucked under an upward curled tongue and then with air applied from the insides of puffed-out cheeks. There seemed more effort to this whistle and it produced a slightly deeper note. Nevertheless it was no less impressive to a small boy who could produce nothing even approaching a whistle whatever the technique employed.

My own later, fingerless, tuneless whistling was quieter, monotonous and entirely unmusical. *I* heard the tunes I was whistling, but no one else did. I could never summon anyone, not even a dog. My attempts to attract someone's attention were feeble and embarrassing, and invariably ended up with me pretending to whistle for the sake of it, gradually lowering the volume before removing my fingers from my mouth, falling silent and walking away.

Later still, I had problems with the valveless cornet in the Scouts marching band, and was just as unable to produce anything recognizable on even that most forgiving of instruments, the kazoo. I was never trusted beyond the triangle or a solitary, closing clap of the cymbals in the small junior school band.

Even as a small boy, I knew that Gloria was a name which suited my young aunty well.

18

M Y father's one true and favoured fraternity during my childhood was the one comprised of the men he encountered in his work and, primarily, in the pubs he frequented. He spoke of these men as though they were familiar to us all.

He left the house three or four nights a week, and regularly on Saturday and Sunday lunchtimes. Invariably, my mother would wait up for him, usually in case he needed a sobering cup of tea or something to eat upon his return. I would lie in my shared bed and listen out for his returning car and then his heavy footsteps down the passageway beneath my bedroom.

When all three children had started school, my mother returned to full-time work, and it was largely her wage, not his, which ran the household; it was why we lived in debt, forever buying in weekly instalments from her catalogues, finances forever stretched and juggled and carefully calculated into the future.

My mother's chief occupation throughout my childhood was working as a typist and clerk for a company that delivered ready-mixed concrete, and I went to her nearby office once or twice, captivated by the mounds of sand, gravel and cement there, the swinging water hoses and the giant mixers loudly churning as they set off from the depot to their various destinations. Her office was a Portakabin raised from the yard and entered by a metal fire escape. It seemed an exciting place to work, raised above the ground like that.

The lorry drivers were covered in powder and water as they deftly manoeuvred their vehicles back and forth among the mounds of sand and gravel. Calendars from the company came home every Christmas with views of the Dorset coast, the Dales, the Lake District, none of which we had ever visited, or planned to.

My father frequently returned from his pubs with the things he had bought there – always a bargain, always improved upon by his alleged bargaining skills – Egypt again; he'd learned how to haggle, see? – but seldom anything we actually needed or could afford.

Bottles of spirit, sides of bacon, clothes, shoes, car parts, pieces of furniture, even industrial canisters of paint, and our one and only oil painting, bought from an ex-prisoner, of a watermill, badly executed and thickly varnished, and pointed out, along with the carriage clock, to every one of our few visitors. Mostly what was pointed out was that it was an *oil* painting, genuine *oil* paint, not a print or a market-stall reproduction, but an *actual* painting, *hand*-painted in *oil*, an *original*. And by an ex-prisoner, no less, someone else my father had encountered along one of his drinking rounds.

It went without saying that most of what my father brought home was stolen – often disguised as end-of-line or stock-clearance or fire-damaged goods. It was that kind of world.

The bacon was cooked and eaten in the days following its appearance because we had no way of keeping it fresh, and every mouthful was praised and its low cost admired. When the industrial-sized canisters of paint appeared, every piece of woodwork in the house turned a toffee-coloured gloss. What did it matter what colour it was when it had been acquired at such a knock-down price? Probably with a few pints thrown in to seal the deal. Ask no questions, hear no lies. Everybody did it, so why not him? You saw an opportunity, you took it. Be a mug not to. So what if it wasn't your colour or size? So what if you didn't normally wear that style of shoe or didn't immediately need forty cans of engine oil?

Even my Nan stole from the places she worked: poorly filled and wonkily labelled bottles of Carling Black Label from the Whitbread brewery; followed later by giant bags of misshapen Liquorice Allsorts from the Bassett's factory. But this, naturally, was never called stealing, not *stealing* stealing, not real stealing; more a perk of the job, careful how much you actually took, never overstepping the mark, blind eyes turned and all that.

On one occasion my father returned home wearing a glossy black leather jacket and carrying several more. My mother was told to hide these, and informed that in a week or two he'd be selling them on to anyone fortunate enough to seize the bargain he would be offering them. A few days later there was a report in the evening paper of a burglary at a clothing warehouse followed by the arrest of a man who worked there and who was already telling the police the names of everyone else involved.

My mother put two and two together and said she wanted the jackets out of the house. My father, also panicking now that the police were involved, took the jackets from their hiding place and left with them in the boot of the car under the cover of darkness. The next day he told us all that we knew nothing whatsoever about any jackets, that they had never existed. Button it, understand? Keep shtum. Least said, soonest mended. My mother lived for weeks afterwards in constant fear of a visit from the police. We had no phone on which to be contacted, which was a blessing. Other men, my father said, had already been visited. So far, everyone was keeping mum. He – we – just had to do the same. A court case was mentioned, prison even. Thousands of other items of clothing had been stolen in addition to the leather jackets.

After several further weeks, the danger, presumably, passed. Some you won, some you lost, that was the name of the game: nothing ventured, nothing gained. Better a pound earned by getting one over on somebody else than by keeping your nose clean, hard work and agreed prices. Better a pound earned which cemented his own reputation as that kind of man.

It was a world in which a man always knew a man who knew another man who had exactly what you were looking for. And if not *exactly* what you wanted, then close enough. And at half the usual price, who was counting? Men held out their hands and said, 'Shake the hand that shook the hand of the man that shook the world.' Men made their whispered deals, spat in their palms and slapped their hands together. Men peeled notes from bundles in their pockets, slowly counted these out and handed them over one by one. And when the total was reached, an additional coin – a shilling or florin or half-crown – was added to the sum as a gesture of goodwill and something to seal the deal. These were war-time babies and children and National Servicemen, grafters, mates, oppos, wheelers and dealers, and men who were all beginning to understand the benefits and disadvantages of their backgrounds and precisely where they stood in the ever-changing world.

The pubs created their own routines. Certain nights in certain places appealed more than others. Some landlords kept their barrels better than others. Some pubs were avoided because a landlord didn't keep his pipes clean. Most of the bars were men-only and did nothing to encourage women to enter them. The few wives or girlfriends who did occasionally insist on accompanying their men were invariably abandoned at corner tables with a glass of tonic water or orange juice while the men congregated at the bar or the dartboard or sat at card tables, revelling in their own company.

There were sometimes older women in these bars, loud and brassy, drinking novelty drinks such as Cherry B or Babycham, and these were always more tolerated than indulged. Older men sat at cribbage boards, silently counting out scores and matchsticks until one of them won his quiet victory and the convoluted, near-incomprehensible game started all over again. The small rooms with their frosted windows were thick with cigarette smoke. Men stood in clouds of this, waving to clear it between them.

The pub my father visited most frequently was called the Brown Cow, close to the steelworks, its rear wall dropping directly into the dark and lifeless River Don, the colour of its water changing daily and its bed littered with discarded grindstones. Weeds and bushes grew along the walled banks and high up the sides of surrounding buildings, many of which were already falling into disuse and dereliction.

The Brown Cow, a lounge bar and a snug, both equally small and identically furnished and served by the one, two-sided bar, catered largely to the nearby steelworkers.

It was the first bar I ever visited with my father when I was almost old enough to drink legally. At ten o'clock each night, at the end of their shift, the steelworkers would arrive still dressed in their overalls and long leather aprons. The men were given tokens to exchange for beer by the steel companies, and each man would slake his thirst with three or four pints in rapid succession. Just before ten, the barman would begin filling glasses and lining these up on the bar so that the workers would not have to wait. After these first few drinks, the men would slow down and stand together in small groups to drink the same again, afterwards leaving the bar on their own homeward journeys.

My father always waited until time was called and then stretched out his final drink for as long as possible before leaving. He parked his car on a nearby piece of waste land and then drove the twenty-minute journey home smoking heavily and complaining about everyone else on the road.

True to his nature, he scorned the wear-a-seatbelt and drink-driving campaigns which had started to appear on the television every Christmas. He knew which roads to take to avoid the police with their speed guns and their breathalysers, how to drive slowly past their well-known ambush points.

Some pubs even sold special mints which you sucked on as you started driving home and which fooled the breathalyser machines. Certain drinks consumed in combination meant that the police equipment could easily be outwitted. If you drank slowly, paced yourself – three pints an hour, say – then the actual alcohol in your blood was reduced faster than it was built up. At the end of some sessions, he would occasionally refuse the offer of a drink – one for the road – because it would take him over the eight pints everyone then considered to be the limit for drinking and driving. Sometimes, he told us jokingly, he drove home along those dark, carefully chosen streets with a hand over one eye to prevent himself from seeing double.

19

Despite the amount of time and money my father spent drinking during my childhood, he did remarkably little drinking at home. It was considered a sign of poor breeding, degeneracy almost, to keep most kinds of drink in the house. A slippery slope. Besides, his pubs were a vital release for him.

My mother in particular would remark on any drink she had seen in other people's homes. Any social drinking which did need to be done – christenings, weddings, funerals and suchlike – was seldom undertaken in people's homes; there was always a licensed room or hall available for rent in most neighbourhoods, and this was invariably the preferred option.

We had no fridge in those early years, and when we did acquire one, with its freezer space made up of a solitary aluminium ice-cube tray, it was large enough only for essentials such as milk and other dairy products. Occasionally, my father would come home with a bottle of whisky or brandy in a box which had been a gift from either his employer or a grateful customer. But this was to be kept and displayed and its story repeatedly told, before it was consumed. As with the carriage clock, the presentation box gave the gift its vital added cachet. And where personal thanks had been given by the customer on a label or card perhaps, then this too was displayed and carefully pointed out.

On the few rare times when the occasion did demand it – one of those family get-togethers, say – then a cheap bottle of whisky would be bought in, along with giant cans of the same draught beers my father and his brothers drank in their pubs. There would be sherry, advocaat and orange squash for the women. Any of them demanding something more celebratory to drink might be given a port and lemon. The sherry and advocaat only existed because a solitary bottle of each was bought every Christmas. The sherry was rich and sweet and lasted the year, rationed out in small, tulip-shaped glasses; and the advocaat, after Christmas Eve, sat untouched and slowly solidifying in the front room on our marble-effect drinks trolley.

Our collection of glasses – mostly stolen from pubs and clubs – was displayed on this little-used trolley. And alongside them, and adding its own note of sophistication and glamour, stood a metallic-red soda siphon. The cartridges for this were heavy and bullet-like, but they performed their miracle of turning tap water into soda water – something you'd actually have to pay for in any of those pubs or clubs. It was a woman's drink, but man's work to produce.

We children were warned of the damage we might cause if we were to mess around with the syphon or its cartridges, and each time the syphon was refilled, we were all exhorted to gather round and to listen for the hiss of gas as the cartridge was carefully fitted and turned, performing its magic. My mother then drank the soda water, either neat or with a splash of lime cordial, and declared it delicious. A jar of syrupy cherries was added to the trolley, along with the small plastic swords needed to impale and retrieve these.

Someone told me that advocaat was made from powdered egg shells mixed with gin. I always gagged whenever I felt even the tiniest piece of shell in my mouth and so the drink held no appeal for me. Besides, it was intended only for women, and then only at Christmas.

My father's self-imposed restrictions on drinking in the house changed when he unexpectedly started making his own wine. Before this, none of us knew what wine was. Perhaps a bottle was somehow acquired every few years, opened, sniffed at, tasted, savoured, commented on and then ignored and forgotten.

He came home one day with large glass jars, plastic funnels and tubing, rubber corks and thermometers. The wine, he told us authoritatively, was made using tins of fruit concentrate, to which water and yeast were added. The giant jars were then placed around the house depending on whether they needed to be kept warm or cool. The mixed liquids bubbled and frothed and were moved from jar to jar along the transparent tubing. Sediments settled and dark liquid turned slowly near-transparent. After a given time, usually no longer than a fortnight, the wine was finally decanted – that was the word – into bottles, where it finally looked like what it was supposed to be. Real corks were then inserted using a cork-inserter and handwritten labels were carefully attached.

In addition to the fruit concentrates, my father announced, wine could also be made from almost anything else – potatoes, turnips, rhubarb, blackberries, even nettles and dandelions. Another kind of magic to rival that of the soda siphon. Not only would we become wine drinkers, and all that that implied, but he himself would manufacture the drink at practically no cost whatsoever once all the equipment had paid for itself. And we all knew what fancy restaurants charged for even a single glass of wine to accompany their already overpriced food. But just as we knew no one who drank wine, so we also knew of no one who had ever been to a restaurant, fancy or otherwise. In fact, I doubt if we knew anyone who – the odd picnic or fish and chip dinner aside – had ever eaten anything outside their own home that they themselves had not prepared.

In addition to the wine, my father then started brewing his own beer. This seemed much safer territory. If anyone knew about beer, then it was him. Giant plastic buckets filled with the stuff. This frothed more vigorously than the wine ever did, and its smell, not being rubber-sealed and controlled like the more precious wine, filled the small house.

The beer brewing lasted only a short time. It might have been better than anything you could buy in any pub in a ten-mile radius – and, again, who would know that better than my father? – but it took far too much effort. And besides, a bucketful only lasted – what? – two or three nights at most. Apart from which, sitting in your own home, in your own chair in front of the television, and with your noisy, disappointing family all around you was too far removed from standing in your suit and jewellery at a bar with your drinking mates eager to hear everything you had to say to them.

The rest of us were relieved to understand this, knowing that an evening with my father out of the house was, as always, far preferable to one with him among us. We had always understood that the wine was something additional to his beer drinking, something complementary, drunk in far smaller quantities and only when the occasion demanded it. It was a civilized event, wine drinking, another marker laid out for everyone to see.

When the first bottle was finally ready to be drunk, my father explained to us that in France, where wine came from, it would take years to get to this point, years. Someone in the home-brewing business smarter than all those French wine makers had invented this process which allowed everyone to benefit. He poured the liquid into a proper wine glass and held it up to the light. He sniffed at it, holding out the glass for my mother to do the same. She told him she could definitely smell the blackcurrants, or turnips, or nettles. It smelled to me like the paraffin we filled our smoking heaters with, but I didn't say this. Come to think of it, perhaps I *could* smell those gooseberries or dandelions.

My father closed his eyes and sipped at the drink. You didn't drink wine like water or beer; you appreciated it; that was probably the whole *point* of drinking wine. He swilled the liquid around his mouth and then swallowed it, pronouncing it exactly right. It occurred to no one to ask him how he knew this. My mother was offered a sip, took one and screwed up her face. She'd take his word for it. He was the expert, she said. Then I was invited to share in the admiration for both the wine and the winemaker who had produced it. The liquid tasted raw and sharp and made me cough. Trust me to spoil it for everybody. I was too young. Wine wasn't meant for children. Wine was meant only for those people who appreciated the finer things in life. He drank more. Delicious. You probably wouldn't get change out of two quid for a bottle of this in the shops, and here he was, making it for pennies. He drank more, studying his handwritten label. Perhaps he could come up with something smarter for the next batch now that he knew what it turned out like.

As usual, something told me that even he – the first man ever – *ever* – in his family to make his own wine was less than thrilled with the finished product. It was obviously exactly what wine was meant to taste like – he'd read the instructions, followed most of them, and then waited not too far off the suggested fermentation time – but it was probably an acquired taste. It would mellow with age, he speculated, because that's what wine did.

And besides, it was still alcohol, so nothing was actually wasted. And if there was nothing else to recommend the drink, then imagine the faces of all those sipping brothers and sisters, sisters-in-law and brothers-in-law when, upon remarking how delicious the stuff was, he was then able to announce to them that he had made it himself.

Like most of his other fads and enthusiasms, the wine- and beer-making was short-lived and quickly abandoned.

From the age of thirteen or fourteen I started to help myself from the scattered jars and bottles, occasionally topping them up with water. I convinced myself that I was drinking and becoming drunk. Perhaps I was. It was a simple matter of wanting to be someone who drank and who was able to drink. Real men could hold their drink. Real men would always have one more. And then one more after that. And if you couldn't hold it, then don't drink it. I might have felt drunk, I might not, but that was hardly the point. I started drinking for the same reason I started smoking – because both events were a leap forward into adulthood, a place where the constant cloud of my father would hopefully no longer settle over my everyday life. The homemade beer tasted even worse than the homemade wine, probably because it had to be consumed in greater quantities, and I could taste it on my breath for hours afterwards. The taste was even stronger when I was in the outside toilet, throwing it all back up and sticking my fingers down my throat to throw up more in the soon-to-be disabused belief that once it was all out I would be perfectly sober again.

20

I PASSED my eleven-plus exam and my life changed. I didn't know it had changed, but it had. I went from one path ahead of me to another. I didn't know I was changing course, but I was; at the time, I wasn't even aware that those other, different courses existed.

Sheffield had six grammar schools for boys in the late sixties, spread throughout the city. I was allocated a place at Firth Park Grammar, known as The Brushes. The school was a twenty-minute walk from my home, along Barnsley Road, uphill all the way there, downhill all the way home, and was a late-Victorian, stone-built, mock-castellated country house which, over the past forty years, had been closely surrounded by the Firth Park council estate.

There were more recent additions to the original building, but, divorced from its surroundings – and surrounded by a high stone wall – the school maintained the appearance of a wealthy family's home, with high, ornate ceilings, room-height windows, parquet flooring and oak-wainscoted walls. Paintings and plaques hung everywhere; staircases were broad and ornately balustraded. Rooms echoed; windows and skylights were filled with coloured, illustrated glass; Latin mottoes hung over doorways; lists of honoured Old Boys lined the corridor to the main hall; antiquated wooden lockers filled every other space. It was as strange to me as a house in a foreign country, and completely unlike anything I had ever visited or even seen before.

A solitary brown envelope created all of this and led me forward. No one we knew had a telephone then, and so my mother arranged a succession of family visits to pass on the good news and to show me off. She made a point of telling all of our neighbours – even those to whom she otherwise rarely spoke and whom she often went out of her way to avoid – that I was now a Grammar School Boy. Every conversation for weeks afterwards was steered toward the fact of my eleven-year-old academic success.

There was some confusion in my own mind about what being a Grammar School Boy actually meant – largely because at Hucklow Road Juniors, where I had been happy and well taught, I had already been drilled in most aspects of grammar. My young mind made no distinction.

Along with the letter proclaiming my success came a sheaf of papers explaining to my parents what they must now do – all the various items of clothing and equipment that needed to be bought, uniform, satchel, pens, pencils, protractors, woodworking apron and sports kit. I had possessed none of these things beforehand, and my mother's pride may have been tempered upon being made aware of the actual cost of my success. But the necessity of the uniform and all it was intended to confer upon the wearer was no doubt made clear to her, and she swiftly accepted and endorsed that cost.

To help with the expensive undertaking of becoming a grammar school boy, the Co-op department store in the city centre provided everything required by the school on hire purchase. I had become overnight a great financial burden to a family where both weekly debts and Friday paydays remained a constant and worrying preoccupation.

I was taken to the Co-op and the list was handed over to the woman in charge. She no doubt indulged my mother in recognizing and then admiring the small genius before her – the one my mother had given birth to. Perhaps this too helped to assuage my mother's concern about the additional debt she was so suddenly taking on.

And so I was kitted out and a weekly repayment calculated, involving regular visits to our local Co-op branch with money and yet another paying-in book.

Each year, in the six-week summer holiday, the same procedure was again undertaken. A metalworking apron might last until I was sixteen, but trousers, shirts and blazers would not. I grew up and I grew outward, and every expansion had its cost.

For my first year at the school I was required to wear short trousers, a maroon blazer and a maroon cap. I had to wear a tie, which I was patiently taught to tie and position at my throat. The list she had been given told my mother precisely how thick the knot was to be and how low the tie should hang. Shoes – of my mother's own choosing – must always be black, socks always grey.

The school badge of maroon and gold, shaped like a shield and with words I had never seen before, was sold separately to the blazer, and needed to be sewn on. There were blazers with the badges already embroidered on the chest pockets, but by buying the cheaper option of separate components and then unpicking and reattaching the badge each year a small saving might be made.

The new blazer felt heavy and coarse – my first ever jacket – and its cuffs reached to my fingertips. My mother was reassured that the first year's costs did not have to be fully paid off before the following year's requirements could be added. I doubt this was any consolation to her.

It was pointed out somewhere in all this alarming information that, in special circumstances, several of the additional items – the football boots, for instance – might be provided free of charge by the school. Various grants and awards were also available for qualifying children. My mother took advantage of neither: to have sought and accepted these small charities would have diminished my glowing achievement and signalled a great deal else to the watching world. If little else bound us together as a family, then we were endlessly aware of that world and its judgements.

Lists of the successful eleven-year-old boys and girls were published in the *Sheffield Star*. Extra copies were bought and carefully preserved. Application forms for bus passes were sent to hundreds, but I didn't qualify because I lived too close to the school. It was expected that on most days I would walk. The exercise would do me good. I could walk through the terraced streets up that long hill and everyone would see that I was a Grammar School Boy.

On the morning we were informed of my success, I went to see all of my nearby friends to share in their own excitement and preparations for the year ahead. Except none of *them* had passed. Even the clever ones, like me. Not a single one of them. A dozen or so boys and I was the only one. My closest friend, Andrew, who lived in a house on the hill overlooking our own, and with whom I had spent most of my waking hours over the past few years, said that he wasn't coming out to play that particular morning. His mother was upset, he said. The woman – she may even have been a teacher herself; she was certainly employed in a better sort of work – appeared at the door and congratulated me on my success. She told me I deserved everything I'd worked so hard for and achieved. Then she told me that I did realize, didn't I, that Andrew and I would not be seeing quite so much of each other from then onward. He would be going to another school, she said; both he and I would make new friends. Besides, she added, most of my time now would be spent studying. Everything she said came as a shock and a surprise to me.

It was true. There had been a sheet among all the information I'd been sent explaining how much was about to be expected of me from then onward, how much homework I would be doing. Everything Andrew's mother was telling me was true. I didn't even consider it strange or unfair that while *she* seemed to understand everything that was about to happen to me – to shape my growing life – neither I nor my mother had any true idea of what lay ahead of us.

As usual, my father played no part in these proceedings other than being called upon to say how smart I looked when I was paraded before him in my new clothes.

Andrew's mother had been right. I left his doorstep that morning and saw almost nothing of him afterwards. Our friendship evaporated, and probably neither of us understood why. My mother, too, told me about all the changes ahead of me, but she remained considerably less certain of these than Andrew's mother had been. I was being given a chance to better myself, my mother said, and anything I did to spoil that opportunity, well, it would be entirely my own fault.

Over the course of the summer we received further information and instructions. I practised wearing my new football boots and wondered what they might do to improve my non-existent footballing abilities; likewise my long, canvas-coloured woodworking apron. I couldn't even imagine what metalworking might involve, aware only that it was what a great many men did in the nearby vast, dirty, smoke- and fire-filled factories.

I learned during that first year at Firth Park that its Brushes nickname came from the brushes of foxes that had once been displayed there, that in its Victorian or Edwardian heyday, long before the encroaching council estate arrived at its walls, the house had been the meeting place of the local hunt. The Old Boys listed on the high plaques had laid down their lives in both wars and their names were read aloud each year at special assemblies. The Latin motto on my badge said something about Honesty and Trustworthiness. It was the kind of boy I was now expected – and against all odds – to become.

21

WE lived next door to Vera and Linda, older and younger sisters, and their eighty-year-old father. Eighty years then was an age beyond belief, especially when reached by working men and women. A small, quietly spoken man, often remarked upon as being dapper: he always wore a black over-coat, shirt, tie and a black beret – which I associated with his great age – and walked with a silver-headed, polished black cane. Every day he went for two long walks, one in the morn-ing, one in the afternoon, returning punctually to the house and his two waiting daughters for both his midday dinner and five o'clock tea.

Linda, the younger of the pair, worked as a postwoman, firstly delivering letters and then in the sorting depot. Unlike her father, she was a loud, excessive woman, a heavy smoker, and given to demonstrations of flamboyance, pushing into our living room, lighting up, dropping heavily into a chair and then bursting into tears and anger at some injustice she had suffered, usually at the hands of her bosses and workmates.

Vera, her elder by around fifteen years, stayed at home and cleaned and washed and cooked for the others. With the exception of Linda's explosive intrusions and the old man's walking, the three of them seldom left their small home, had no visitors, and seemed to us to be near-reclusive in their habits.

When we saw any of them over the low wall which separated our back gardens, we stopped to talk to them. Neither Vera nor Linda had ever married. Nor did either of them have any friends, let alone men friends. In Vera's case, we assumed that this was because she was older – a true spinster – and because she was devoted to looking after their elderly father; and Linda because she was forced to work all the hours God sent to support the three of them, however frugal their shared existence.

After five years of living so close to them – they were the only neighbours we occasionally heard through our joint walls – the rumour arrived suggesting that all was not as it seemed in that cloistered, inward-looking household. Linda, it was whispered to my mother – and here she again warned us to be careful about what we repeated – least said, soonest mended, and all that – Linda, it was whispered, was not Vera's younger sister, but was in fact her *daughter*, conceived and born out of wedlock.

This sudden understanding, however imperfect, however unproven, explained everything. Thirty-five years ago, the baby Linda had been born and all of their lives had been changed and then set along the single, shared course ahead of them. A story had been concocted and stuck to. It was why they were all as they now were; it explained everything.

But to us, a family with its own carefully maintained and self-regulated fictions and deceits, it changed nothing: to us they went on being father and daughters. What difference did it make? What business was it of anyone else's? my mother said. But illegitimate children were still then a hammer blow to every supposedly decent family, where both fitting in and keeping up appearances remained of paramount importance.

One Christmas Eve, Linda brought a bottle of sherry into our house and insisted on my mother and father sharing a drink with her. We knew all about her sporadic excessive drinking by then, and we tolerated it along with her other excesses. She seemed to me to be a woman forever trying to break out of her old, restrictive skin, and she intermittently achieved this with her loud, disruptive, and occasionally offensive, appearances in our home. She had nowhere else to go. She insisted on my mother fetching our best glasses, poured the sherry to the brim and then drank most of the bottle herself. My father considered sherry a woman's drink, and so drank little. Besides, in an hour's time he would be off on his own celebrations.

After an hour, Linda fell asleep where she sat. And an hour after that, she woke with a start and, to my mother's relief, insisted on leaving immediately. Her sister and father would be worrying, Linda told us. Every time she left the house, she said, they wanted to know both where she was going and when she would be back. It was only natural, my mother told her, already holding the door open. I remember it was snowing and that the snowflakes were blowing vigorously around the two women and into our small warm kitchen.

22

As my mother's weight increased she started wearing a girdle – a cylindrical contraption of fabric and stays and rubber with clips for stockings attached to its lower edge. This restored something of her former figure, though only a little, and it was clear to everyone who knew her that the battle she was waging with her increasing weight was being lost. Her hair remained thick and black and her complexion dark and smooth.

She only wore the girdle when she left the house, either to go to work or to the few family events we attended. She complained good-naturedly that the contraption didn't allow her to breathe properly, but that this was a price worth paying. The first thing she did upon her return home was to remove the girdle and then tell us all how much better she now felt. It was another of the many burdens she had to bear. She was only in her late twenties and early thirties when this daily rigmarole took place, and her weight then and forever afterwards became an unhappy and restrictive burden for her.

She complained of having large bones, of a slow metabolism, of only having to look at food to somehow gain its calories, but the photos of her slim and attractive youth belied all these delusions. She prepared five meals two or three times a day, and anything eaten outside the house – our packed lunches, say – were invariably made by her before her own departure for work each morning. She worked in a cramped and under-equipped kitchen and often ate as she cooked.

To attempt to counter her weight gain, and when the girdle became too painful for her to bear, she embarked on endless diets, chief among which was replacing the sliced white bread we ate with crispbreads; and meat with cheese, particularly cottage cheese, which was considered a guarantee of weight loss. Adverts on the television and in her women's magazines showed slender women borne into the air in hot-air balloons eating small slices of brown bread, and so this too was bought, stretching her small budget, and kept carefully apart from the white sliced loaves which remained a staple for the rest of us.

We favoured Fletchers bread over Mother's Pride, partly because of the price, but also because Fletchers loaves came wrapped in yellow and white striped waxed paper, which opened out into a sheet when the bread was finished and which could then be used for days afterwards to wrap our sandwiches.

Breakfast, dinner, tea. Supper, on the rare occasion it appeared beyond closing-time social events, comprised a hot drink and two biscuits. Never more than two, and usually with the suggestion that if there was anything fancy in the biscuit tin, then only one of these was to be taken. The more costly biscuits were invariably bought and reserved for whenever rare visitors were due to appear.

My mother told us to chew our food. We were not allowed to speak with our mouths full. We cleared our plates – not merely because we were usually hungry, but because there were always starving children elsewhere in the world who would be glad of what we left. We ate separately from our father, whose meals continued to be delivered to him in his chair, on a stool, beside the fire, in front of the television.

Arriving home from school each day, we children usually prepared our own meals and ate these before my mother returned from work. Instructions were frequently left for me to light the gas beneath a pan of waiting potatoes or to bring the pressure cooker up to steam before my father's return. He, following his own routine, would arrive home punctually at ten to six, go upstairs to remove his shirt and tie and wig and then reappear as his food was laid before him. An hour would then pass – the national news followed by a soap opera – before he went back upstairs to prepare himself for going out again.

Ever conscious of his appearance, my father started taking so-called slimming tablets after every meal. These, we were told as we were warned away from them, would counter whatever the person taking them had just eaten; it was something scientific to do with metabolism – something as little understood by him as the rest of us. The tablets were vividly orange and identical in shape and size to Smarties. Tea followed by tablet followed by six or seven pints of bitter and an end-of-night whisky.

One year, a tanning lamp appeared in the house and we were all positioned in front of its violet-coloured glow to reap its benefits. Goggles like plastic bottle tops were positioned over our eyes and held in place by an elastic strap. As further protection, we were told to sit with our eyes firmly closed. Someone always timed these sessions, and along with the other rules of use, these strictly observed timings further validated the lamp's benefits.

My father was always careful to take off his wig when using the lamp, forcing him to use the thing in his bedroom. The rest of us sat in the eerily lit kitchen, naked to the waist. The goggles left white circles around our closed eyes.

The rays of the lamp, in addition to helping improve our overall well-being, were supposedly good for acne, blackheads and yellowheads, pinhead-sized spots which my mother searched out assiduously and quickly squeezed. A child with blackheads and yellowheads was a child from a dirty home with parents who didn't care. Hair nits were regularly combed out and snapped between my mother's thumb- and fingernail. Ears were checked for excess wax, fingernails for dirt, and necks and wrists for tide marks.

There was always somebody to point a finger and judge, always someone in authority waiting to pounce on our failures or indiscretions. We were poor and often struggling to keep up, but we must never appear poor and struggling to the world. My mother always insisted on clean underwear and socks every few days. What would happen, she asked us almost daily, if we were to be knocked down by a bus and taken to hospital? What would the ambulance men, the nurses and the doctors think of us then? Even worse – what would all those people think of our mother, of the home we had come from? It always seemed a fair point to make. And it was always a *bus* waiting to knock us down and force us to reveal our dirty underwear and unwashed necks to the world, never a car – all those additional watching, judging passengers adding weight to her argument. In contrast to my father, who thought only of himself, my mother loved us and cared for us by these admonitions.

After a week or two, the rest of us abandoned the ultra-violet health lamp, whereas my father sat at his carefully timed sessions for years afterwards. As good as a holiday, he told us, but none of us could ever possibly agree with this.

23

I STARTED delivering papers when I was thirteen. Every morning and evening, thousands of other boys and girls across the city did the same. The paper shop was on Popple Street, little larger than a kiosk, divided in half by a hinged counter, and with every small space stacked with magazines, sweets, cigarettes and an array of cheaper toys, mostly Matchbox cars, Airfix models and jigsaws. A sheet of yellow plastic hung in the window, supposedly to prevent everything inside from fading in the sunlight.

The man who owned the shop often arrived there in darkness to take delivery of the bundles of papers, drag them inside, cut the string which bound them, and then, using his round-book, build up one route per bag, pencilling in the street names and numbers, slipping smaller papers into large papers and magazines into these. Most households had two deliveries a day, often consisting of several items each.

The weight of the bags was almost more than many of us could carry, and we were always keen to start lightening our loads. The morning deliveries were mostly tabloids and quick to deliver. Letter boxes were slender, intended mostly for letters and bills, and whenever a larger paper was ordered, especially one with supplements, several minutes were spent dismantling the load and flattening these for the too-small slot. Customers came to the shop to complain that their papers were torn, but no one took these complaints seriously. We were kids; the news might be good for half a day; who cared?

The delivery routes moved out in a circle from the shop in all directions. Routes often crossed and ran in parallel along opposite sides of the same street. Most doors faced immediately on to the pavement, and these were always the preferred rounds. Larger houses often meant a gate and a driveway, and more often than not one of the thicker papers at the end of that extra walk. The routes on the steeper hills, zig-zagging up cobbled slopes, were invariably given to new-comers. Men on their way to work told us where they lived and we found their papers for them, and sometimes they tipped us for this.

We were all half-asleep and the papers were usually delivered by rehearsed routines rather than by studying the pencilled street names and numbers. Sometimes the papers were grabbed by dogs and there was some fun to be had by pulling the delivery back and forth and provoking the animal. Some boys brought carts to carry their loads; others arrived with shopping trolleys and were laughed at. The bag I carried on my back bent me double for the first half an hour. For many of us, these were our only forays into these nearby but unknown neighbourhoods.

We encountered our rivals from other shops and shared complaints. We swapped stories of seeing naked women, or women at the door in their see-through nightgowns, none of which were true. I delivered to a large house called Page Hall, and embellished the stories of the ghosts which haunted its overgrown grounds.

Tales and rumours of ghosts were a common and much-appreciated feature of all our childhoods, and especially those related to the war. The best known of these was that of the twenty or so ghosts haunting the vaults of a popular city centre department store, used as an air-raid shelter, but which then received a direct hit from a German bomb. Perhaps it was even something my reluctant grandfather had witnessed or at least heard as he stood above the city on one of his lonely, terrifying watches. There was always a connection in my young mind.

The paper shop owner tolerated no complaints from us. The filled bags covered his small floor. We arrived, were told which one to pick up, and to start walking. Occasionally, he would give us a sweet or a piece of chewing gum, let us take a drag on his cigarette or pull down one of his top-shelf magazines for us to look at before we set off out into the empty streets. Most of the shop's customers were working men going back and forth from the mills, forges and factories of the nearby steelworks. All bought a paper, cigarettes and often those sweets which were considered medicinal, keeping their chests clear and their throats lubricated against the heat and smoke in which they worked. They bought fishing magazines and magazines about cars they would never be able to afford, and they flicked unashamedly through the same pages of naked women before deciding which one not to buy.

My favourite delivery routes were along streets like my own, where the houses were close together, and where doors faced each other only a few feet apart along the tunnel leading to the back yards.

There was extra money to be made by delivering on Sunday morning, and by taking round the racing and football papers late on Saturday afternoon. Men who had missed the results round-up and who had pools coupons to check were desperate to learn the final scores and we were frequently promised a share of their hoped-for winnings.

Once every few weeks, the more trustworthy of us were sent on rounds to gather in all the money that was owed. Most customers came into the shop to do this and were given dated ticket stubs as receipts. When these stubs built up over a month we were sent out with the tally books to collect payment at the door. Most people on most rounds ran constantly in arrears and the shopkeeper accepted this. If people didn't have the full amount owed, he told us, then at least take something off them. It was a kind of contract and everyone involved understood and honoured this.

Once, one boy returned to the shop as my own takings were being counted and told us he'd been beaten up and robbed. His face was bruised and his nose and lips were bleeding. He was crying uncontrollably, more in fear than pain. The shop owner took him into the back room and let him wash his face, telling him he'd survive. The police were called and presumably arrived later in the day.

I asked the boy a week later what had happened and he told me that a man had told him to come into his house while he went in search of his wallet, and had then threatened him with an air pistol unless he handed over the cash. When the boy had done this, he was punched in the face. Tell anyone what had happened, he was warned, and he'd get the same again the next time he turned up at the door. He said the man who'd punched him had also let him wash his face and stem his bleeding nose and lip with a towel before letting him go.

At Christmas we were given tips, all of which were intended to be shared out on Christmas Eve. The shopkeeper gave us all presents – usually boxes of celebration chocolates which could no longer be sold. Matchmakers were a great novelty and favourite, better appreciated than the far-too-sophisticated After Eight dinner mints. Terry's Chocolate Oranges were similarly coveted, and in our house they were always associated with Christmas; to eat one at any other time of the year seemed wrong.

The Sunday papers often featured lurid tales of paper boys and girls who had been murdered or abducted, or worse. Or tales of paper boys who had witnessed crimes or who had averted some impending disaster or other. There were famous cases of paper boys who had been killed by armed robbers simply because they were out and about so early in the morning; boys who had disappeared in the darkness of a winter dawn never to be seen again.

My morning round dictated that I leave our sleeping house at quarter past six, run to the shop, complete my deliveries, return my bag, run home, eat my breakfast and be out of the house by quarter past eight to get to school twenty minutes later. It was always a tight schedule. My father complained when he heard me using our indoor toilet and so I stopped using it. In winter, when the outdoor toilet was frozen solid, or beyond a foot of snow and ice, I went down into the cellar and pissed into the mound of coal beneath the grate.

Eventually, my father's sleep having been disturbed once too often – and how many warnings did I think I was going to get? – he came downstairs one morning just as I was about to leave the house and told me to tell the shopkeeper that it was the last time I would be turning up. I wept at the prospect of losing the job and at letting the shopkeeper down like this. But my father insisted, laughed at me for crying like a baby and went back to his bed. That night, upon his return from work, he behaved as though nothing had happened. I'd been delivering papers for over three years by then and was one of the most senior and trusted boys, able to pick and choose my routes and to pocket most of the tips I was given.

I had grown to despise my father long before this particular incident, but his reaction that morning seemed particularly unfair and malicious to me. He laughed again when I complained of having no money and told me I should have thought of that before I'd woken him up and deprived him of half an hour's sleep. Besides – here we go – when he'd been my age he was already working full time and handing over all his wages to his mother; I didn't know what real work was. The fact that I was crying like a baby told him everything he needed to know.

24

THE Watsons lived at the bottom of the street, close to the shop. Paul, the eldest, was my age. Both his parents worked full time and he too was left in charge of his younger brothers and sisters, of which there were three or four. Even as a child I knew that Paul Watson was something of a fantasist. Every day he arrived at the club car park or whatever other piece of waste land had been chosen as our playground with yet another tall tale about himself or his parents.

His father had won the pools and they would all soon be moving to a much larger house in a better part of the city. He was going to leave school and take up a well-paid apprentice-ship somewhere. The Army or Navy were sending him letters begging him to join up when he came of age. He had an uncle who worked for the city council and who was going to improve all their fortunes in the near future. His father had been offered a job at three times his current wages in Manchester or Leeds or somewhere. He wasn't sure where.

His younger brothers and sisters often appeared alongside him and stood as surprised and disbelieving as the rest of us at hearing these tales. Some of them even believed him and wanted to hear more. He, naturally, resented their presence and all they might afterwards repeat to their parents. Perhaps he told them everything was meant to be a surprise – one they would ruin by repeating. Perhaps he confessed to them that he was making everything up because he considered their family to be unjustly caught amid the rest of us. Or perhaps he genuinely believed everything he was telling us. Whatever his motives, few of us rebutted these far-fetched tales or asked him for proof. We had as little contact with his parents as he had with ours, and so, once told and briefly discussed, all these fantasies evaporated into the same air we all breathed.

Paul Watson's biggest fantasy, and the one he told most often, was that he was about to undergo a special operation – no, a *series* of special operations – to make him taller. He was too short for his age, we could all see that. We could see, too, that his legs were thin and bony and that they bowed outward slightly at his knees, causing him to walk with a gait and to run awkwardly. We were less scornful of this particular tale, and sensing that there might be at least something behind the fantasy – his legs *were* misshapen, he *was* too short – we indulged him in it.

He was going to have metal pins fitted into his leg bones which would stretch them. Not for him the clumsy leather and metal callipers worn by others; he would have actual operations to straighten his legs. The metal pins would somehow be lengthened. The heads of special screws made of a brand new kind of metal would show through his skin.

When all this finally started – any day now – he'd show us, *then* we'd believe him. And when we saw all this and were forced to admit that he'd been telling the truth all along, perhaps then we'd also have to reconsider all his other hitherto unbelievable tales.

Special doctors were already considering his case. Famous men his parents had already met and spoken to. He was one of only very few children being offered the treatment which would normally have cost thousands of pounds to undertake. And everything was free because he was such a special case. He had already started visiting the hospital to have his legs measured and his walking studied. X-rays had already been taken.

It was important to start soon, he said, while his legs were still growing. Leave it too late, and his bones would be fixed unalterably in their crooked shape. Leave it too late, and all those doctors and surgeons would have to start looking for another patient to perform their miracle on. And when all this did finally get under way, he'd be absent from school for months, perhaps even a whole year.

We all knew that Sheffield was ringed with special hospitals – isolation hospitals, mostly, out on the rim of the Peak District in all that healthy air – and Paul Watson would be cared for in one of these.

When the operations began, it would be a long and painful process. But worth it. The doctors had already asked him how tall he would like to finish up. There were already predictions of how successful the operation would prove to be. All the doubts in the minds of Paul Watson's audience were quickly and confidently batted away. What did we know? We hadn't been there when he and his parents had gone to see the doctors. We hadn't been there when all the measurements and X-rays had been taken.

And so we listened to Paul Watson's stories and we encouraged him to show us where his leg bones would be straightened and strengthened, where the screws made of that rare and precious metal would protrude through his skin, where the curvature of his legs would be corrected, and how the recon-figured limbs would leave him tall and straight and walking normally.

And those of us who might still doubt him – even in the face of all those experts and their important decisions – well, we could think what we liked. We'd be the ones looking stupid when he came back from the hospital taller and stronger than any of us.

He even said he'd started taking boxing lessons in a nearby gym, where proper boxers trained, and who were showing him how to start looking after himself in readiness for that new life ahead.

In fact, when it was all over and done with, he said, and when everyone was congratulating themselves on how success-ful everything had been, he would probably continue with that boxing training and become a professional boxer himself. Plus, his father had once been a boxer. In the Army. A champion, in fact, and they had a mantel full of trophies – solid silver, mostly – to prove it. When we asked to see these, he laughed at us and asked us if we'd ever heard of burglars. The mantel was filled only on special occasions, family get-togethers; the rest of the time the trophies were kept well hidden.

Sometimes, Paul Watson said, the local paper sent a reporter and a photographer to their house to interview his father and to print photos of the medals and cups. The next time this happened, he said, we'd all be warned in advance and we could go and watch. Everything Paul Watson continued to tell us, he revealed to us as though he were doing us a great favour and as though we should all be grateful to have him at our centre.

25

Two or three times a year my mother took us to the cinema – the pictures. The Essoldo, Sheffield Lane Top. A short bus journey to a vast building covered in white, blistering stucco, steps rising to a foyer, scarlet carpets and gold-painted furnishings. A pleasure palace built and perfectly positioned at the heart of the vast Parson Cross housing estate.

The evening paper listed all cinemas and everything they showed throughout the day. Most offered a double bill of films supplemented by cartoons and newsreels. We would be in place by half past six and seldom back out into the night until four hours later. Our usual bedtime as young children was half past seven, rising to nine o'clock as we reached our early teens. Staying up late, staying *out* late, was a significant part of the cinema treat.

The films we saw were rigidly certified and we would not have been allowed in to watch anything deemed unsuitable for children, even accompanied by our mother. My mother would keep us close, buy us drinks in paper cups, and then ice creams from the tray-women who paraded the aisles, and who also sold cigarettes and chocolate. The vast room would quickly fill with smoke, vividly apparent where it rose in plumes through the shafts of projector light, changing colour as it went.

A velvet curtain hid the screen until the first film was due and then the two halves of this drew apart with a fanfare as though in an actual theatre. Pearl & Dean adverts showed us nearby stores and, even more excitingly, nearby Indian and Chinese restaurants where we might one day go for a meal after walking back out into the cool night air.

My mother told us about her courting days with my father, many of which were spent in similar picture houses, which afforded them their rare moments of privacy, comfort and darkness.

Our biggest thrill was to be alone with her and out of the house. My father never wasted his money on the trips – wait a few years and the film would turn up on the television for free – and, besides, we would all have resented his presence. To be alone with my mother, and on such an exciting excursion, was all we craved. She showed herself to us in another, unfamiliar light on those occasions. She was in charge. She took control. She was the one making all the decisions. She paid for our fares and tickets and sugary treats. She talked to the people we met. She introduced us to them. We felt an asset to her, an achievement almost. It never mattered to me what films we saw; they were all memorable because the occasion itself was memorable.

Because my brother was six years younger than me, even if I'd been, say, fourteen, he would only have been eight, and my sister eleven, so our actual choice of films was restricted to this age group. Our choice was increased on the occasions we were considered as 'accompanied minors' – another small excitement.

We sat in the darkness, mostly in silence, gripping our plush seats in anticipation of all that was to come. Sometimes, watching a film determined to scare us – pirates swinging across rigging in rough seas, a giant snake crawling across a jungle floor toward a playing child, an armed villain hiding in a shadowy doorway – we held hands. Audiences breathed in unison, gasped and cried out together. It was all another part of that shared pleasure.

My mother, too, enjoyed the rare experience of being out of the house and alone with her children. My father wasn't there to tell us to stop making a noise, to stop showing off, to stop showing him up, to stop making fools of ourselves. We were aware of the need to be home before his own return, but that was the only constraint he imposed upon us on those precious evenings. There was a bus terminus next to the Essoldo and a succession of buses would arrive to coincide with the end of each night's programme.

The city centre cinemas showed films throughout the day and varied their programmes more frequently than the Essoldo. But the Essoldo was our chosen place, and too much rested on our need for those nights to remain exactly the same for us to take a dangerous risk and go elsewhere. Besides, the bus journey was a short one and could be properly planned. We were invariably home before my father – his own timings, as always, calculable to the minute: last orders, drinking-up time, chucking-out time, noisy farewells, the drive home, traffic, getting parked, home.

26

DURING my first year at grammar school I became friends with a boy called Terry. He was the only boy I knew whose parents did not live together in the same house. Terry lived with his mother somewhere toward the city centre, but once a week he came close to where I lived to have tea with his father and older brother. These two men lived and worked together as foundry men, and their small, crowded house possessed no comforts or mod-cons apart from a television. The two men made a great deal of Terry's arrival, always waiting for him with a present, the promise of a future outing, usually a football match, and with precisely the same meal of chips and two fried eggs week after week.

Terry asked me to go with him on several of these visits. We arrived straight from school in our uniforms and carrying our satchels, and we left at a specified time so that Terry could catch the agreed bus back to his mother. He told me she would always be waiting for him at the bus stop to quiz him on the visit. She, he said, insisted on calling him Terence.

The two men fussed around us, trying to show an interest in what Terry and I had been doing at school that day. We showed them our books and whatever work we had undertaken, and they shook their heads at the cleverness of it all. They told Terry they were proud of him and exhorted him to learn as much as he could. Look at them, they told him. Was that how he wanted to end up? It wasn't, but neither Terry nor I said so. The two men may have understood little of what Terry and I told them, but at least we appreciated their feigned interest, enthusiasm and encouragement. They told Terry he was creating chances for himself that neither of them had ever imagined existed.

We showed the men our homework and they laughed and shook their heads. Piles of newspapers stood around the room, along with all the other detritus of their untended lives. Terry told me his mother asked him about the state of the house each time she met him. The hearth in the room in which we ate our chips and eggs was filled with ash and kindling. Our chips were cooked in liquid beef dripping in a saucepan, our eggs in dripping in a frying pan. Doused in sauce and vinegar, it was a delicious meal. Terry told me he sometimes made up other meals to tell his mother about.

When we left, the two men gave us both money, often emptying the change from their pockets into our cupped hands as though it were nothing.

I never met Terry's mother, but I guessed that her life – and her grammar school boy son's with her – was far removed from what it would have been with the two men.

Sometimes, when the time to leave drew near, Terry's father would smother the start of tears and then be reproached by his eldest son. Terry's father admonished Terry to work hard at his schooling and to get all his certificates, or whatever they were called these days. Terry was embarrassed by all this, as was I, though probably for different reasons.

Outside, when the visit was over, Terry and I would wait at the bus stop together and divide equally the money we had been given. He sometimes told me to take it all and to return his share to him at school the following day. Sometimes he came as close to tears at the bus stop as his father had done in the house. I was embarrassed by this and pretended nothing had happened, which suited us both. I possessed neither the understanding nor the sensitivity to say or do anything helpful, and so I laughed at him for being soft, after which, in the way of boys, he laughed at himself for the same thing.

I learned very little about Terry's other life with his mother, and nothing about what had broken the family in half. I envied Terry, knowing how much better, how much more bearable my own life would be with the removal of my father. But in truth, the possibility of this was unthinkable. Families were families, they were what they were, they did what they did, you got used to it, you put up with it, and in that way everything was kept exactly where it belonged. A family that could not maintain itself and its boundaries was a shameful thing and something to be avoided at all costs. And so I both envied Terry and I pitied him.

After a year of these visits, Terry left the school and all contact between us was lost. I assumed his mother had moved house, remarried perhaps, and that Terry had moved to a school closer to his new home. There were those five other grammar schools and so, presumably, having earned his right to be there, Terry would have transferred to one of these. And so he went and I never saw him again. Whatever was happening, it was no longer any of my business.

A year after Terry's departure, I started delivering papers to the houses on either side of where Terry's father and brother lived, and when the football season started I took the sporting paper to their own home, always careful to push it silently through the letter box and be away from the house before either man came to the door and recognized me.

27

I STARTED going fishing when I was twelve or thirteen. Someone gave me a rod, reel and wicker basket and I was quickly seduced by the tackle shops and their arrays of brightly coloured floats, their endless varieties of lead weights and – most dramatically of all – by the fish-shaped lures and spinners: iridescent silver and blue minnows, cast out and then retrieved through the depths and then across the shallows, their bait-mimicking motions caused by their brass swivels and propeller-like fins. If nothing else, then at least these useless accessories looked like small, actual fish on the end of my all-too-often empty line.

I bought an expanding tackle box – an elaborately hinged contraption which opened out into a succession of clear Perspex drawers, every one of which I filled with all these bits and pieces. Most of the time I used only tiny lead shot, minuscule hooks and porcupine quill floats. Maggot, hook, shot, float. Cast out, adjust float depth, sit, watch, wait, sit, watch, wait. Every five minutes I would reel in my line in the hopeful expectation of there being something on the end. More often than not, my maggot would be missing and I would interpret this as having had a bite or a nibble, a near miss. With each cast, doubt would fill my mind regarding whether or not the maggot was still down there wriggling enticingly on its hook. Older men told me to suck the maggots to liven them up, but I never did.

I became friends with several other fishing boys and we went off together most Sundays. Coach companies ran anglers' excursions from the city centre, departing at five and six in the morning. These ran out into the Peak District and down through empty, green Lincolnshire all the way to the Fens. We were dropped off, shown where to go, left for the day and then picked up and brought home eight hours later.

I spent whole days at deep, dark mining- and mill-ponds, and at small Water Board reservoirs. I sat on the steep, man-made banks of the Welland and the Nene and caught a hundred gudgeon, every one of them weighing less than an ounce. On the days when our floats never moved, we switched to those seductive spinners and annoyed the more experienced and patient anglers with our constant splashing.

The more committed fishermen possessed landing nets, keep nets, umbrellas, rod stands, catapults, ground bait and mechanical and battery-powered sensors which picked up the slightest twitch of their rods' slender tips. I bought whatever I could afford of these gadgets, but my catches remained disappointingly small or non-existent. I bought fluorescent floats and bite indicators for dark mornings. I went night fishing with my friends and we sat in the dark and the cold on our wicker baskets struggling to see what we were doing.

We fished in ponds ringed by slag heaps where nearby drinkers watched us and then laughed at us and wondered aloud if anyone had ever caught a fish in the last twenty years where we now sat and waited.

Men fired balls of ground bait into the water with their catapults and we cast our own lines as close to these as we dared. Men told us to fuck off and to stick to our own fucking swims. They told us to fuck off and to stop fucking spoiling things for everybody else.

These serious anglers became angry when they were denied their usual swims by these impatient amateurs, early at the river bank or pond solely as a result of the bus timetable. Men arrived with giant flasks filled with hot drinks, foil-wrapped sandwiches, pies, sausage rolls, Scotch eggs, teacakes. Men brought bottles of beer or walked back and forth between nearby pubs.

Occasionally, local youths showed up selling fresh bait. For years, I bought wasp grubs at so much per precious grub because I was convinced that these were the guarantee of a good catch. The serious anglers used luncheon meat, sweet-corn, moulded bread, and rubber baits which resembled shrimps, and which they doused in pungent oils.

My collection of floats and lures expanded by two or three pieces every Saturday. A stall at the open air Sheaf Street market sold everything in individual pieces. Floats designed for every occasion cost pennies each and often appealed to me more than the possibility of all those fish waiting to be caught by them.

Not all my expeditions were fruitless – alongside the limitless gudgeon, there was often one or two small silvery roach, eels or perch to be caught – and so I persisted. There was always something exciting in that tug of a living thing somewhere in the depths, something unseen and waiting to be revealed. I enjoyed the friendship of my companions and the grudging camaraderie of the men who tolerated us and taught us. I enjoyed the various locations to which we were delivered, some in the countryside proper, some amid the industrial wastelands, working mines and black, girder-lined canals which surrounded Sheffield for twenty miles in every direction.

Catching a single one of those silver wriggling fish was enough to make me continue making the effort for months afterwards.

Older, I came home after a Saturday night out, got changed and went off to catch a night bus back into the city centre. I kept all my fishing equipment in the outdoor toilet. Occasionally, I would return home unable to get into the house, and knowing what would ensue if I woke my father, I would get changed and then sleep in the toilet until it was time to leave for the early-morning bus.

My father told tales of his own fishing expeditions as a child, though I doubted these. Owning even the basics of the hobby cost a small fortune.

On one occasion, when I was fishing at Ecclesfield pond, behind yet another working men's club, my father and two of his drinking friends turned up with glasses in their hands. He'd known I'd be at the pond, and he came up the stone steps leading to the water calling to me. Everyone turned. The pond was ringed mostly with boys my own age. The more experienced anglers knew how little of any worth the water contained since the closure and then destruction of the mill to which it had once been attached.

My father and his friends came to where I was sitting. He asked me how many I'd caught and then shook his head at my answer. I was probably doing everything wrong. Why was I sitting down? Why was I using that float and not another? What size hook? As usual, I wasn't making nearly enough effort. What was in the water anyway? Roach, I told him. A few perch. The usual, plus a few eels. What about trout? he said. It was a myth of the pond that a giant trout had once been caught there. The story varied. I devoured countless magazines and manuals on fishing and I knew where trout lived and how far out of reach they were to anglers like me.

I told him it would be impossible for a trout to live in the pond. But that was my problem, see – I knew everything and nothing. I was desperate for him to leave, for him and his friends to finish their drinks and to go back inside for more. I was fishing, and this was part of my life and world that he had never previously invaded.

But instead of returning to the bar, he put down his glass, took my rod from its rests and reeled in the line. And then, his cigarette still stuck to the corner of his mouth, he started swinging the line with its float, weights and baited hook back and forth like a fly rod. I asked him what he was doing. What *I* should have been doing, he told me, instead of all this sitting around, eating sandwiches and getting fatter. What *I* should have been doing if I'd had an ounce of the sense I'd been born with, which I clearly didn't.

He went on like this, making a spectacle of himself, until the line caught in one of the bushes behind the path. He pulled at this but it was firmly stuck. Line spooled loosely from the reel and lay all around him. Along the bank, boys started to smirk and then to laugh openly. My father pushed the rod back into my hands and returned to join his friends, who were by now waving their empty glasses at him. At least he'd *tried*, he said. At least he'd used his initiative instead of just sitting there.

He finally left and I was relieved to see him go. I laughed with the boys alongside me, and it occurred to me then that this was another of those instances when, unable to resist showing off, unable to resist trying to prove that he knew better than everyone else, my father had once again revealed himself in his true colours.

I saw this often enough in the confines of our home, where he ruled unchallenged, but this was one of those rare occasions where others had been witness to his irresistible need to dominate, to prove himself better, more capable or knowledgeable than everyone around him.

It had always been a given in my father's life that he was more intelligent, capable and knowledgeable than most men; certainly than any woman or child; and certainly than anyone *younger* than himself. It was what forever compromised, and then eventually undermined him both as a husband and as a father.

I carefully retrieved most of the line, cutting it free and discarding that which was knotted and tangled. I retrieved my precious float and resigned myself to the loss of the weights and the hook. I tackled up again and then sat for the rest of the afternoon happy to watch my motionless float drifting on the lifeless water.

I started to calculate what might happen when I eventually returned home. If I left this late enough, then he would have slept off his dinnertime outing and might already be launched on his usual evening trajectory. The next morning would be a working day and a school day and so, as usual, our paths through that same world and routine would remain largely separate and apart.

By the time I reached seventeen, fishing began to lose some of its appeal to me; besides, there were other demands on the little money I earned. Others among my friends also lost interest and so, with nothing else to bind us together, we drifted apart. At the end of one season, I put away my basket and rod in the outside toilet and left them there.

Months later, told to clear them out of the space and either sell my tackle or throw it away, I opened the basket to remind myself what I possessed. At the base was a large, square biscuit tin in which I had kept my maggots in their pungent sawdust. These would all surely have been dead by now. I rested the tin on the toilet seat and prised off the lid. Inside lay a block of fat bluebottles, mostly dead, but some still alive and causing the black mass to spill out over the edges of the tin. None of the creatures could actually fly; instead they seemed only to expand slightly upon this exposure to the light and air. The sudden stink of them made me gag.

The flies flowed like slow lava onto the toilet seat and bowl and then dripped to the floor. I panicked and dropped the tin, scooping up the living and the dead insects and what remained of their foul-smelling sawdust and flushing everything down the toilet. My mother called from the kitchen door to ask me what I was doing. Nothing, I shouted back. Flush after flush after flush, until most of the pulsing black mass was finally gone.

I put a card in the newsagent's window and a man turned up one evening, said the rod, reel and basket would be perfect for his own son, told me I was asking too much for it, offered me a much lower price, told me it was all I could expect, take it or leave it, he was doing me a favour, and then left with everything I owned. I followed him out onto the street and saw the boy waiting in his father's car, his head craning out of the window with excitement.

28

THE working men's club was the focal point of the street. It was one of the largest and best attended in Sheffield, and despite the drawbacks of having the place so close to where we lived, we took a kind of pride in this. A brick-built block with no ground-floor windows, and a broad metal fire escape running up its side to the first floor. Every Wednesday, Saturday, Sunday dinner and night the club put on turns – singers, comedians, impressionists, novelty acts and, occasionally, on Sunday dinner, female strippers. By climbing the fire escape it was possible to look through a small dirty window into the corridor leading from the dressing room to the wide stage.

The club had a reputation for the high calibre of its entertainment, and men came there from all across the city to watch this. When a television celebrity was performing, there were queues along the street an hour before the doors were opened. The fact that these entertainers had indeed appeared on the television featured boldly on all the advertising posters. Expectations were raised even further by an appearance at either the London Palladium or at a Royal Variety Show – men and women who had actually appeared and performed in front of the Queen. And now here they were, those same men and women, singing exactly the same songs you heard and saw on the radio and television and telling the same risqué jokes only *six doors* away from where we lived.

When there was no Name act, one or more of countless local singers, comedians or groups would fill the bill, often all three. In a room of a thousand drinkers, everyone listened, laughed and applauded together.

Very few turned up at the Club, even on weekday nights, dressed in anything but their best suit. There was a dress code, rigorously enforced by a Club committee, a member of whom always sat guard at a table in the foyer. Guests of members were allowed, but only after going through the ritual of having been signed in by that *bona fide*, sub-paying member. Men and women from other, affiliated clubs arrived and were admitted. Some people even followed the better-known acts from club to club, where they might be found performing six or seven nights a week. Bus timetables were calculated to disgorge and then gather up these vast audiences.

Like their husbands and boyfriends, the women who came to the club took the same opportunity to show off their finest, newest and most fashionable clothes. Most wore headscarves to protect their sculpted, lacquered hairdos. Artificial fur coats and high-heeled shoes seemed obligatory most nights.

It was always a shock to me to see women the same age as my mother behaving drunkenly, laughing and shouting and arguing with their husbands as they made their way home at the end of each night. Odd lost shoes, glasses and scarves were frequently scattered along the pavement the following morning, along with money dropped as drunken men had pulled on their coats against the cold or rain.

Sometimes, and especially when a band was performing, the small car park would be filled with lorries and vans delivering musical equipment, which was laboriously manhandled inside through a high metal door at the rear of the building. Boys would gather to watch, asking unsuccessfully to be shown what lay inside the guitar- and drum-shaped cases.

Sometimes we would see the performers themselves, waiting outside, smoking and drinking before they were called in to perform. The better-known acts were occasionally delivered to the club in a chauffeur-driven car, creating a spectacle of their arrival, and further heightening the sense of occasion which already filled the street outside.

On calm summer nights, the singers and musicians could be heard the length of the street, and certainly through the open window of the bedroom I shared with my brother. I always imagined that the windowless ground floor of the Club was designed to prevent anyone who hadn't paid their subscription catching sight of the performers. 'The Green Green Grass of Home', 'Is This the Way to Amarillo?', 'Anyone Who Had a Heart', 'Hey, Big Spender', 'Delilah'. Songs we all knew by heart.

The occasional strippers were announced as Gentlemen Only events. Sunday dinnertime, twelve till two. After which men, forced to drink their fill quickly during those restricted hours, would stagger off home to their waiting dinners. It was why our Sunday dinners were invariably eaten later than those of other days – at two, say, rather than the usual midday.

A blue comedian would often compère for the strippers, and the combination was a popular attraction. We always knew when the place would be filled and the street congested.

Once a year, the Club organized a trip to the seaside – usually Mablethorpe or Skegness – for the children of its members. Early one summer morning, a line of cream-coloured charabancs would line up along the street and children would be checked on board. We never went on these trips and they were always a thing of great envy to me. I crouched at my bedroom window looking down into the street and the gathering crowd there, careful not to reveal myself.

The children on the bus were given a large bottle of pop, a bar of chocolate and a bag of crisps for the journey, along with money to be spent upon arrival. This was always fixed in my mind as thirty shillings, a vast amount for a single day.

One by one the coaches would fill, numbers counted, names checked, sweets and drinks handed out – and then proudly displayed by their recipients for their watching parents to see – and the buses would move off in convoy to cheering and applause. After which, the early-morning street was suddenly silent again. All the parents dispersed, leaving only a few committee members consulting the clipboards they held, before they too moved away. It was said that they went to the club, where a free breakfast and drink awaited them.

Later, long after dark, and long after we had been sent to bed, the coaches returned and those same parents and committee members would gather again to disembark the lucky trippers. Just as I knew of the treats and money that had been handed out, so I also knew that the whole convoy had stopped on its way home at a roadside eatery where everyone had been fed fish and chips, all previously arranged, and again all absolutely free of charge.

Sometimes, men coming out of the Club into the cold night air after four hours of drinking would relieve themselves or throw up in our tiny front garden or in the dark shadow of our passageway. Their voices and the noise of their pissing and vomiting could be heard inside. My father was usually out himself when this was happening, and my mother would wait until the men had finished and walked off before going out and swilling away whatever they had done there with a stiff brush and a bucket of milky, disinfected water.

29

As girls, my mother and her sister looked like twins. But as they got older, Joan grew taller and less fine-featured than my mother. Joan became good-looking, my mother briefly glamorous. They both had the same lustrous, jet-black hair which remained long into old age before greying. Both women gained weight as they aged, but being taller, Joan was always better able to carry hers. Joan, who gave birth to five daughters, the oldest three our contemporaries, remained more or less the same shape all her child-bearing life.

Joan married Stan, a tall, dark, handsome man who was a sailor when she met him, and who appeared in his uniform with his beribboned cap, flap-collared tunic and bell-bottom trousers in several family wedding photos. A sailor at a wedding was considered a portent of good luck and future fortune.

Joan and Stan and their daughters lived in a semi on the edge of the Parson Cross estate, and with a garden which ended at a slope of rough pasture with a beck at the bottom. Travellers' horses roamed the unfenced slope and came to the garden fence. This illusion of rural life was further enhanced by the name of the cul-de-sac on which the house was situated – Strawberry Gardens.

Upon leaving the Navy, Stan began work as a travelling salesman for a firm selling Sheffield Steel products. Unlike my father, Stan was often away from home, staying in commercial hotels and using trains as well as driving himself. He entertained other company men in restaurants and bars. He had an expense account, something no one else in the family had ever possessed. Stan then started travelling in Europe, Germany in particular.

My father, as was his way, made disparaging remarks about Stan, just as he made them about his own brothers and brothers-in-law. There were remarks about the company Stan was now keeping and the amount of time he was away from his home and growing family. A wife and five children, and yet *still* he preferred to be gadding around and sleeping and eating out. And we all knew what that led to. Plus there was the fact that Stan had once been a sailor, and we all knew what *that* signified, too. It was clear to everyone, even us children, that Stan loved his wife and daughters considerably more than my father had ever loved either my mother or us. Stan came and went – occasionally for weeks at a time – and every time he went away there was always genuine unhappiness in Joan's household. And then, when he returned, there was great joy. The girls doted on their father; they missed him when he was away and spoke excitedly of his expected return. He came back with gifts for them all. He bought them toys and clothes from abroad, sweets and bars of chocolate with strange names. He bought Joan a machine for peeling and chipping potatoes – a boon in a family of seven, where potatoes were bought and consumed by the sackful.

Stan returned home on one occasion with cartons of German cigarettes in his luggage – cigarettes made not of tobacco, but of lettuce leaves. Yes, *lettuce*. Completely safe to smoke. The shredded lettuce was black and stank as it burned, but there the cigarettes were, a gift for us all. Stan was the only person I knew who had flown on an aeroplane, and this further enhanced the man-of-the-world image I created of him.

The burden of raising her daughters was Joan's alone, and, again, I knew how much happier I would have been if a similar arrangement had existed in our own home. My mother's love for her children – and ours for her – was forever compromised by her being forced to position herself between us and my father – something which, inevitably, altered her own relationship with the man, leaving none of us any the happier or feeling any more secure.

The tales and rumours about what Stan got up to while he was abroad grew – tales that were whispered in our presence, and which we were warned against repeating because of the hurt it would cause to Joan. And like all rumours and open secrets, these were first corrosive and then destructive. My father took great pleasure in all this. At least *his* marriage was to all intents and purposes a good one. Ask him, he'd always known Joan and Stan would end up like this.

Eventually, Stan and Joan did separate, and then divorce, and Joan stayed at home with their daughters, while Stan disappeared back into the world he alone had inhabited. To give him his due, Stan continued to support his family, but he now lived largely apart from it.

And now that he was fair game, the tales of Stan grew even darker. Everything added up: my father had been proved right, had been right all along; if only people had listened to him.

The eldest daughter told me they now all hated their father for what he had done to them, but her voice belied her true feelings. Some of the younger girls denied everything that was now being said of Stan. I myself believed little of what my father said; I knew all too well by then how his tales and suggestions were tailored to suit his own vindictive ends. I couldn't remember a single instance of anyone being as excited or as happy about the return of someone as those girls had been about the return of their father from one of his trips abroad. Stan, my father said, had become too big for his boots. In that family, the higher you climbed, then the further you had to fall – and, rest assured, fall you would – and the further you fell, then the harder you would land. It was another of those lessons for us all.

Stan may have returned to visit his wife and daughters after their separation, but I never saw him again. When I asked why he had gone, I was told that there was every good reason for his departure and that some things were best left unsaid.

Any argument that Stan had once loved his wife and daughters and that he had treated them well and provided for them all those years hit the solid wall of his sudden departure. If Stan had been completely innocent of all he was accused of, then why had he gone, and gone so swiftly and completely from their lives? And because he had gone, and thereby confirming all my father's suspicions, then further embellishments might now be legitimately added to all those whispered tales and rumours. My father might not be the perfect husband or father, but he was better than *that*. He might not have done half the things Stan had done for his children, but at least he was still *there*, still playing the family man and keeping everything in its proper, rightful place. *We* wouldn't be living with the shame of separated parents or an absent father. *We* wouldn't be forced to listen to such embarrassing, shameful tales and pretend not to care. *We* wouldn't now have to forget everything a good and loving and reliable father had once been to us and then learn to despise the man as we tried to live our lives without him.

Joan, still a handsome woman as her girls all grew into adulthood and then supported her and gave her grandchildren, never took up with anyone else, never even considered it. She'd had her fingers burned, see? Be grateful for what you've got, remember where you came from. People had long memories; she'd do well to remember that.

30

S TRANGELY, perhaps, I have few vivid or lasting memories of my younger sister and brother other than those of the annual or family events in which we all participated: two more small children amid many cousins. My sister was three years younger than me, and being a girl, inhabited a different world entirely. My brother, six years younger, was mostly an annoyance and a restriction to me, the two of us being forced to share a bedroom, first in a double bed and then, when I left junior school, in bunk beds, which my father constructed from a pack, and which creaked and swayed each time my brother climbed to the higher level. Only the two restraining walls kept the beds unsteadily upright.

My brother was twelve when I left home at eighteen, and so remained a child, a small boy, to me. Neither my brother nor my sister attended school in Ecclesfield. Afterwards, following our move toward the city centre, my sister came to the same junior school and I was made to walk with her to and from our home.

I was always the clever child in the family, and this too created a divide between us. Following me through my younger schooldays, my sister and then brother were often compared unfavourably to me and this fed resentment on their parts. My brother arrived at the junior school just as I left it for the nearby grammar. He told my mother that all the teachers expected him to be as well behaved and as hard working as I had been. My sister echoed the complaint. In truth, I possessed neither of those qualities to any great degree, but forever afterwards the remarks echoed. They were endlessly compared to me, they said, and usually found wanting. The accusations were thrown at me as though I had deliberately engineered the comparisons and had then benefitted by them at their expense. It took the edge off my own rare achievements.

We couldn't all be clever, my mother told them, hoping but failing to convince and reassure them. My father continued to take no interest whatsoever in our education. Getting a good education had been far from a priority in his own hard young life and it hadn't done him any harm, so why should it bother us?

It annoyed me to see that, by the time he reached his own early teens, my brother suffered little of the vindictive behaviour and humiliation I had endured at my father's hands at the same age. My father – still not yet forty – seemed to me to have changed. My brother was already far more practical than I had ever been, good with his hands, interested in applying himself to the world around him rather than retreating from it, as I did; he was interested in cars, for instance, in how they worked and performed.

My brother left junior school and attended a Secondary Modern. I learned the basics of wood- and metalworking. I built a hallway hat-rack for our hallwayless, hatless family, and a tea caddy spoon for measuring out loose tea leaves just as we abandoned this in favour of teabags. My brother talked of engineering and apprenticeships, of getting the necessary licences to drive different classes of vehicles. His aim was to train himself and do everything necessary to start earning a proper wage as soon as possible, and in this he was successful. He left school at sixteen with few qualifications and went to work in a steel mill, followed by a job as a lorry driver, followed by establishing his own haulage business. Living away by then, I took little real interest in any of this.

My sister, because she came more regularly into conflict with my father and his ideas of how children should behave toward their elders and betters, bore the brunt of his anger. However ineffectually and disappointingly, from the age of fifteen or sixteen I started standing up to him, and so he turned his attention to the child he could continue to control, and upon whom he might yet impose the severest of his strictures.

At fourteen or fifteen my sister started dressing up to go out with her friends. She started wearing make-up. There was talk of boys forever hanging around. Not boyfriends, exactly, but boys all the same, drawn to her because she was attractive and because she sought their attention, approval and affection. My father could see where all this was leading. He would insist on inspecting her before she left the house. He frequently instructed her to change her clothes for something more decent. She wore too much make-up. Where was she going? Who with? He always wanted her back home earlier than she had hoped for. When she argued with him he told her to get upstairs and to forget about going out. And besides, why did *she* think she could swan off with her so-called friends like a little tart when her mother was exhausted from working all day to put food on the table and still with a pile of washing and ironing to do? As usual, my mother would attempt to intercede and say that she didn't mind. Of *course* she minded, my father insisted. In fact, now that he thought about it, why didn't my sister help out more around the house? If she wanted to be treated like a grown-up, then it was time she started behaving like one. It was an all-too-familiar argument to us all.

By this point, my sister would be crying, the prospect of spending time with her friends, and going somewhere for the simple pleasure of being out of that house and with others, over. She cleaned and swept her small bedroom. She washed the kitchen floor. She could argue and sulk as much as she liked, my father told her; it would get her nowhere. While she lived under his roof, she obeyed his rules. If he told her to do something, she did it. My mother might protest further, just as she had protested on my own behalf, but my father's power and control over his family remained absolute, and whenever he felt this power to be threatened, however indirectly or unintentionally, then *all* our lives were made unbearable.

On the rare occasions I did answer my father back, he laughed at me, threw a few slaps and then told me that *I* knew where the door was just as well as my sister did. Minor conflicts quickly escalated. My father's cruelties, large and small, seemed an even greater pleasure to him as we grew, and his arguments, as ever, continued to be manufactured out of nothing. His simple understanding that the one who shouted the loudest or threatened violence won the argument continued to hold fast.

Why didn't we just listen to him? Why didn't we just do what we were told without any backchat or sullen looks? Why didn't we do it more willingly? Why didn't we do it without endlessly having to be told? Why didn't we think of other people for a change? Why didn't we use *this* – his knuckles rapped hard on our skulls – once in a while? Why didn't we surprise him, why didn't we use our own initiative once in a blue moon, why didn't we stop behaving like children? Did we know how old *he* was when he'd lost his father? Did we know how old *he* was when he'd been forced to leave school and go out and earn his living? Well, *did we*? Did we know what would have happened to *him* if he'd behaved for a single moment how we were behaving now? Any attempt to answer these questions drew him into an even greater rage.

At some point in all these depressingly familiar arguments he would invariably ask us how old we were. And when we told him – ten, say, or thirteen – he would shake his head and say no – we might *be* ten or thirteen, but we were actually in our eleventh or fourteenth year. Eleven or fourteen, not ten or thirteen. Older than we thought, so why didn't we act it? Did we know what *he*'d been doing when *he* was ten or thirteen? No, of course we didn't. What did we think? Did we think this world owed us a living? Did we think there weren't millions of people out there who weren't exactly the same as him waiting to get their hands on us? Were we going to behave like this to our bosses? In front of the people in the factory where we'd end up labouring? We needed to start working a few things out. Who did we think we were? And if we didn't believe him, then we just had to wait and see. And if we didn't like the way things were, then, again, we always knew where the door was. I was always my own worst enemy in that household.

I would occasionally leave the house at being told this, and then spend a few hours walking around and wishing I'd been less rash. Perhaps I thought I was punishing him. All that would then happen was that I'd wait for him to leave in the evening and then go back into the house. The following morning he'd laugh at me, telling me I'd proved him right in everything he'd said. Where had I gone, had I been cold, had

I cried, had I felt sorry for myself, had I had time to consider my behaviour and the error of my ways? Was there anything I wanted to say to him? But whatever I might have said in reply to any of this, he would only laugh again and say he didn't have time to stand around listening to my pathetic excuses. Some of us had work to go to. Somebody had to buy all that food we ate and keep that roof over our heads.

When he had gone, my mother told us to ignore him. No one had come to any real harm; no one beyond the five of us was any the wiser. It was just him being him. We should all know better by now. Just agree with everything he said and do everything he told us to do. Why make life harder for ourselves? Things were bad enough already. If he said black was white, then we should too. After all, what real harm did it do?

31

G OING to the grammar school imposed an order on my life I had never before known. A full timetable regulated my days there. But more importantly, the school created for me an environment in which, for the first time, the months and years ahead of me started to come into sharper focus. It was an all-boys' school, the teachers all men, and for the first time in my life I encountered dedicated, approachable, professional men who talked to me in anticipation of an answer, who actually asked for my opinion, and who then considered my answers and gave me their honest response; and men, moreover, who occasionally and good-naturedly conceded that even a wrong or guessed or ill-judged answer had its value.

It was a considerably stricter regime than any I had encountered before, and most infringements of school rules were punished in some way. But these punishments were seldom unjust or unwarranted. Whole classes might be punished for the misdemeanours of a single boy, but this too contained its lesson and had its positive effect on me. No punishment exceeded its crime. And certainly no punishment was capricious or excessive or likely to turn to physical violence at some uncontained and exasperated point along its trajectory.

Those men who were strict and demanding were also encouraging and supportive. When I could not grasp something – mathematics was forever a blind spot – those men explained things over and over to me. Where I succeeded and then embraced the novelty of all these new subjects so suddenly within reach, I was praised, rewarded and pointed out to others as someone who was doing well, doing his best, making the most of things. Languages, chemistry, geography, history, art, literature, biology, physics.

I showed my mother my full, eight-period daily timetable, to which was added homework. I gave her the note which explained how important it was for me to be provided with a quiet and private space in which to do that homework. But peace and solitude were rarely achieved in that busy household. If there was someone at home, then the television was invariably switched on, often in competition with the transistor radio on a kitchen shelf.

I was proud of all these new subjects, and I explained in great detail to my mother what each of them was. She was certain I'd do well in them all. For her, too, all that mattered was that I did my best, that I *tried*.

To my surprise, I came top of the class in German, and in the top three for geography and art. I was in the bottom three for maths and Latin, but in my mind these two extremes balanced each other out. In a family where any kind of academic achievement was rare, I made the most of my successes. After all, you couldn't have everything.

I went daily into a near-stately home of oak wainscoting, parquetry floors and high, decorated ceilings. I was given my own personal locker, for which I bought a flimsy lock and a golden key. A fountain pen salesman visited the school and we all bought pens, deciding there and then whether to use ink in bottles or cartridges. I chose the latter solely because of the warnings I had received about getting ink on any of my new, as yet unpaid-for uniform.

Early punishments included detentions and line-writing – convoluted sentences, sometimes in another language, where correct spelling and punctuation were always insisted upon. Other boys, apparently, led me astray, and I did the same to them.

There were prefects in the school and these older boys drifted around the rooms and corridors forever gathering up miscreants and delivering them to receive their punishments. A discussion would then take place, during which the boy – me – would be asked whether or not he considered the punishment justified and proportionate. Boys were given the chance to explain themselves and to offer apologies.

For the whole of my first year, I was convinced that I was unworthy of the school and that I belonged elsewhere. I lacked all confidence in myself. Soon, someone in the Education Authority would see that a mistake had been made and I would be transferred elsewhere, presumably to the concrete and glass Secondary Modern less than a mile away, where boys went for a few years before moving on – at best, to an apprenticeship; at worst, directly to one of those noisy, dirty, overheated factory floors.

But instead I started to do well; I was encouraged and I was praised. I was constantly told that I stood as good a chance of making something of myself as any other boy in the school. I was told my home circumstances and upbringing had nothing to do with it. I was shown that application, dedication and simple hard work led to worthwhile results. I was never told that I was a failure. I was never allowed to feel sorry for myself at finding myself so suddenly out of my depth and in such unfamiliar surroundings. I was told that it was up to me – and to no one else, no one else whatsoever – to make a go of things.

My termly reports said over and over that I found it difficult to apply myself, that I messed around and showed off in front of my friends. This was a pity, they said: I clearly had brains but didn't yet know how to fully apply myself. When I saw the point in studying hard, then I did it; when I failed to understand something, I invariably played the clown. My father read this on one report and repeated the mockery – class clown – for decades afterwards. Our son, The Class Clown. What did they expect? What did any of them expect?

I made many friends in the school, but our friendships existed only in school. These boys lived all over the city and I never visited their homes – partly, I knew, because I could never invite them to mine. They spoke of their own families, their own parents, in ways I never could, or dared. From the very start of my time at the school, I was grateful to be able to keep these two halves of my existence completely separate.

My father might have continued to dominate the house, but my days at school were beyond his reach. I was careful to only ever deliver good news to my parents. I could hide detentions and line-writing. Any letters home I could tear up and then lie about my parents having read them. I became even more adept at signing my mother's careful signature on sick notes.

I took in the small amounts of money required for trips and events and these placed an additional burden on our small budget. When I finally started earning money at Saturday jobs, my father told my mother that I would be paying for my own trips and treats from then on. She gave me the money from her purse anyway and warned me against letting him know. When my father questioned her, she lied to him, just as we all did.

My mother attended every school parents' evening with me in tow and listened to all the praise and gentle criticism aimed at me. She agreed with everything that was said. She was doing all she could. My father was unable to attend, she said – the closest she ever came to an outright lie – but she promised to relay to him everything she'd been told. I had a bright future ahead of me, she was told, and she took considerable pride in her part in that future.

As in all things, neither of us told my father anything other than what he wanted to hear, keeping him at that vital, necessary distance. He, in turn, boasted to his drinking friends that I was a grammar school boy. Your father tells us you're a grammar school boy and that you get your brains from him. Stands to reason. *He* could have been a grammar school boy if his life had been easier, if fate and necessity hadn't intervened, if there had been any fairness whatsoever in the world. He's an intelligent man, your father; you can tell that just by listening to him talk; he knows things you won't find in any book. You could tell how proud he was of having passed these brains on to me, they said, by the stories he told when he was buying and accepting drinks. But there were always two sides to that particular coin: Latin? What was that when it was at home? Physics? Proper little Einstein. Biology? Cutting up dead rats and worms? What was the point of that? Still, fair play to me, these men said: use the brains you've inherited and stay away from hard labour. Brains, that's what counted in this world. Runs in the family. Must do.

32

T HE oldest sister was called Valerie – always Val – and
she bore much of the burden of bringing up the family
of six children following the early deaths of their father and,
a few years later, their mother. Val was twenty-one when the
younger children were finally orphaned.

Soon after, Val married Arnold, a bus conductor, and the
pair of them continued living in the family house at the centre
of the council estate. Val and Arnold had two sons, neither of
whom I saw much of. Arnold was a gentle man who came and
went from his work in his uniform, leaping fare-free on and
off the buses which passed their home.

My father mocked Arnold's quiet manner and pitied him his
obedience to his wife. Arnold helped with the daily chores; he
drove a small car and took his family on outings; he delivered
his wife to the shops and the city centre and then helped her
with her shopping before driving her home again. He wasn't
really a drinker, Arnold, and he knew hardly anything at all
about football or cricket, cars or darts or all those other manly
things that filled my father's life.

In his spare time, Arnold made models – plastic kit models
and balsa wood aeroplanes, covered with tissue paper and
painted with dope which stretched their skins taut and shiny.

Some of the planes even had small engines and petrol tanks to fuel them. So fastidious and committed was Arnold to his hobby that he frequently adapted the kit models, making new parts for them out of sculpted plastic and then painting on carefully researched identification insignia instead of simply applying the ones provided by the manufacturers. Arnold even painted faces on the small, rigid figures sitting in the cockpits.

I coveted the models, and occasionally Arnold gave me one to add to my own clumsily constructed and badly painted collection.

On my own models, the glue showed, neither propellers nor wheels actually turned, and Perspex canopies and gun turrets were painted over. Transfers were clumsily and unevenly applied, and many tore and twisted as they dried.

On Arnold's perfect models even the bands of the metal frames of gun turrets were painted, along with additional logos and lucky charms on the fuselages. There was a whole room in Val's house given over to Arnold and his model-making. According to my father, it was something Arnold should have left behind him when he and Val married, a childish thing. I saw in Val that she admired her husband for being different. And perhaps what pleased her most was that he was unlike her own three brothers.

Val was the sister who most resembled their beloved mother. She seemed old to me even as a young woman, and certainly much older than her two younger sisters. She wore old-fashioned clothes, usually buttoned-up cardigans and pin-afores which stretched from her neck to her knees. She looked like the woman holding up my arms in that solitary photo of me and my grandmother.

Gloria, the second sister, was the acknowledged beauty of the three, with plenty of make-up and long, curly auburn-blonde hair. She possessed enough confidence for all three girls. She always spoke the loudest and behaved the most outrageously. Gloria stood her ground. She wore fashionable clothes. She argued with other women in the street; she even argued with men, including her eventual husband, brothers and brothers-in-law. You had to watch Gloria.

Gloria had boyfriends who rode motorbikes and wore black leather jackets. Tearaways. She needed to be careful. She needed to watch herself. If anybody in the family was going to the bad, then it was Gloria. You never knew what she'd be up to next.

Gloria eventually married Judd – a common abbreviation for George; just as Jack was for John – one of her motorcycling, leather-jacketed boyfriends, with his Brylcreemed, jet-black, duck's-arse haircut. She rode pillion round the housing estate on his motorbike with him, a girl without her mother and father, a girl still carefully watched over by her three older and overprotective brothers.

And then, years later, Gloria and Judd separated and then divorced. It was the family's first ever divorce. Hundreds of years, as far as anyone knew, generation after generation of happily married families doing their duty, keeping their marital noses clean and their heads down, and then this.

Gloria, bold, ambitious and headstrong as ever, took everything in her stride and built a new and happier life for herself.

She went to live on the far side of the city, away from the vast estate favoured by almost everyone else. Some in the family may have pitied Gloria for her waywardness, for never being satisfied with what she was given, for never completely and unquestioningly accepting her lot in life. Others, I imagine, envied her her self-created and hard-won freedoms. Gloria lived her life halfway between that of her older sister, Val, who had become a mother to her, and her one-year-younger sister, Mary, over whom she herself exercised a kind of parental dominion, and who often seemed to me like a daughter to her.

Mary was always considered the baby of the family. She was calm and academically motivated where none of the other five showed any such inclination. And, perhaps because of the way Gloria was turning out, she was kept the most firmly under the watchful, protective eye of her five older brothers and sisters.

Mary was eleven when I was born, and thirteen when her mother died, and consequently she was the one raised longest and closest in the family of her siblings. Thus were the generations, the families and their losses and gains conflated and made continuous. The girls mothered Mary, and the three older boys formed close around her. Among this network of love, concern, protection and censure, Mary was always spoken of as the one true hope of the family. The year I was born, Mary passed her eleven-plus exam and won her place at Abbeydale all-girls grammar school.

Mary continued to live with Val in the family home. As predicted, she did well at school, and then afterwards at college. She started work in Sheffield City Department of Education – as highly regarded among the city's inhabitants then as its Housing and Highways Departments – and became the family's first true professional. She met David, another employee of the Department, and together they became a new direction for the family. Perhaps, despite all his disparaging remarks about David and education in general, even my father was pleased for, and proud of, Mary.

Mary and David got married and took out a mortgage on a house. I was at the wedding as a ten-year-old page boy, rubbing his fists into his eyes in the solitary group photograph where everyone else stood grinning stiffly.

Mary gave birth to two children soon after the marriage and we saw even less of her and David. The pair of them attended the usual obligatory family gatherings, but mostly they lived their lives separately from the rest of us in a home we never visited.

Later, when I was in my mid-teens, Mary became ill with a cancer which moved eventually and untreatably into her lungs, and following whatever treatments she was given, she was finally taken to the hospital at the top of our road. The family again closed its ranks around her. The youngest of them all, only twenty-seven, married six years and the mother of two small children. And the only one of them who had never smoked when most of the rest of them had smoked like the proverbial chimney all their lives. So where was the justice in that? How was that fair? And where was God in all of this? Why did other people smoke and drink and go to the bad and then get off scot-free? And why did people who lived blameless lives and set examples for others all around them have this happen to them?

My father raged over the death, they all did, at the down-right unfairness of everything that had happened to their baby sister. The world echoed for years with all these questions. What woes and problems did we, his own family, suffer and endure when compared to this? It was another of his delib-erately unanswerable questions. To even attempt a response was unthinkable.

When Mary died there was a further fracture in the family, something else irretrievably lost. We saw almost nothing of

David and the two small children, and it was made clear to us that there was another family out there – David's parents and his own brothers and sisters – whose responsibility it now was to take charge of David and his motherless sons. Ties were slackened and then severed, and David and his children spun off into that other orbit.

It started to become clear to me that there were forces considerably more powerful than my father's will operating in the world, and that none of us were immune from their effects – forces over which even he had no control and which left him as useless and as impotent as the rest of us. Mary became the lost sister, the lost child, the lost baby. She may have become a wife and a mother late in her short life, but after her death she became a child again. And the world became an even more hostile, unfair and unforgiving place.

33

ONE morning my father called me up to him where he
sat at the dressing table looking at the polystyrene head,
over which his precious hairpiece remained carefully draped.
There'd been a bit of a cock-up, he told me, and the vital double-
sided adhesive tape, which usually came through the post,
hadn't arrived. Someone, he said, would have to pay a visit to
the Crown Topper Agent in the city centre to buy some more.
Someone trustworthy, someone who could be relied upon to
go straight there and back, get the tape and keep shtum about
everything.

He handed me a sealed envelope and told me that the name
of the tape and the money for it were inside. It was such an
important errand, he said, still watching his reflection over the
polystyrene head, that he would drive me into the city centre
himself and then wait for me while I carried it out.

The address he'd written on the envelope was the name of
a barber in the Castle Market, a place I knew well, and which
immediately struck me as not being a fitting place of business
for the prestigious, high-end people of the Crown Topper
organization.

He took me to the market entrance and dropped me off. He'd
circle around, he told me; parking close by would be impossible.

I went into the crowded building and found the barber's. I'd never visited the place – my own barber was much closer to home – because every time I'd passed it on my visits to the market, it had always been full of old men, smoking heavily and usually studying the racing pages. They were there now, and most of them looked up at my arrival. The barber, perhaps believing I'd entered by mistake, asked me what I wanted. I asked him where the Crown Topper Agent was, and he smiled. Everyone smiled. Some of the waiting men nudged each other, lowered their papers and watched me closely. The barber took the envelope from me and deftly opened it, quickly pocketing whatever money it held. Have a look in there, he told me, indicating a drawer close to the shop window. Every surface was covered with the old men's fine shorn hair.

The drawer had a label sellotaped to it marked 'Crown Topper'. I opened this to reveal the scattered rolls of tape, combs, scissors and other bits and pieces with which I was already familiar. Can you see what you want? the man asked me. The comb and scissors in his own hands never stopped shaping and snipping at the head in front of him. I picked out a roll of the vital tape. He told me to take two.

Then he asked me who the tape was for, and because I'd already been primed to tell him that the buyer was a bona fide registered Crown Topper customer, I smugly told him this, and he immediately took offence at the evasive and dismissive answer. Have it your own way, he said. My uncle, I said, suddenly and inexplicably reluctant to tell him that the wig-wearer was my own father. It's his uncle, the man announced to his watching customers, breaking into a smile and causing them to laugh and then to cough.

I closed the drawer and made my way to the door. You want to tell your uncle to come back to me direct for anything he wants, the barber said. I'm half the price of the Crown Topper mail order people. I wondered if my father had anticipated getting two rolls of the precious tape for the money and I decided to keep one of them. In all likelihood, he'd run out of the stuff sooner than expected because I'd been cutting pieces off the roll to stick up posters and pop magazine pages in my bedroom.

You want me to put that in a bag for you? the barber asked me. Discretion, and all that. I told him not to bother. The words 'Discretion Guaranteed' were plastered all over the Crown Topper brochures my father occasionally received. Now, having visited the public arena of the firm's so-called agent, and felt the amused, watching eyes of his customers, I saw yet another of the company's proud boasts for what it truly was.

As I passed behind the barber, he stopped his cutting for a moment, turned and laid the palm of his hand on my head, twisting it slightly. Don't worry, he told me, you can't see the join. Even more laughter and coughing. I felt myself redden. Another wig-related indignity or embarrassment to add to the growing list.

I left the shop and wandered back out into the bustling market. Traders shouted from all the stalls – fruit and vegetables, fish and meat, mostly, but with stalls selling tripe and cow heel, cheap greeting cards and wrapping paper, second-hand books and magazines, including my own Commando comics – buy for half the original price and then trade in against another for half of that. They were clearly rapidly diminishing returns, but still a bargain to me.

Back down in the street, I searched for my father, but saw no sign of him. He appeared a few minutes later, flashing his lights and gesturing for me to go to him where he waited, unable to get any closer to the kerb. I gave him a single roll of the tape and he asked me if there had been any change. None, I told him. Typical, he said. They know you're in a fix and so they do that to you. He waited for a gap and pulled out into the traffic. At least now I knew where to go, I told him, hopeful of further visits and more free tape. Not at those prices, he told me. In future, he'd make sure to get his order in early. Nobody took *him* for a mug, he said. At least not twice they didn't.

34

I NEVER played any sport with the slightest degree of skill, enthusiasm or even interest. The grammar school, however, was keen on all kinds of character-building, competitive activity: P.E. twice a week and alternate Friday mornings of swimming or football, rugby or cricket, an annual cross-country run. I dreaded them all in equal measure.

I never learned to swim. On my first outing to the swimming baths, my pale, flabby body on show, I clutched my chest and stomach and wandered with the three or four other non-swimmers to the shallow end of the pool. Even there, the water still rose midway between the flab of my stomach and my small breasts. Everyone else was lined up at the deep end and was pushed in one at a time to great hilarity by our enthusiastic sports master. And everyone then bobbed back to the surface laughing and gasping and spitting water at each other.

Over at the shallow end, we were told to climb out of the water, to walk to the deep end and to do the same. How difficult could it be? Swimming was more of an instinct than a sport. Newborn babies could swim, for God's sake. How ridiculous would we non-swimmers feel – what shame and embarrassment – if one day we fell into a pit pond, a mill leat or a dirty canal and drowned there? Poor lad, he couldn't swim. What do you mean he couldn't swim? Everybody can swim; even newborn babies can swim.

Everybody, we were told by the sports master, could swim, whether they knew it or not, and now was our chance to prove it. We lined up close to the man, and without warning he pushed us into the deep end of the pool. We sank to the bottom and some of us stayed there, struggling to glide smoothly or fishlike to the surface, our mouths open, filled with heavily chlorinated water. My baggy trunks started slipping down my thighs. The only idea inside my head was that I was going to drown. And then a long wooden pole started to probe the depths, clumsily striking us and prodding us upwards.

We all eventually rose to the surface, gasping and sputtering and clutching frantically at the lip of the gutter which ran around the pool, and where we then hung, breathless and frightened and desperate not to lose our grip.

The floating, splashing swimmers laughed at us again, encouraged by the man who had just been proved wrong, and we four or five failures were told to pull ourselves toward the ladder rising from the pool and then get back to the shallow end, where we belonged; we may have let ourselves down as usual but, once again, we certainly weren't going to be allowed to spoil it for everybody else. When those others came swimming smoothly among us, we were all careful to move out of their way, almost as though we were doing them a favour.

Where P.E. was concerned, I became adept at signing my mother's signature on forged notes. Verrucas. A skin infection. Gastric upsets. Dear Sir, my son has been feeling bilious of late. I had every confidence in the notes, especially when sealed in an envelope. I was told I didn't look unwell and to get changed anyway. If the worst came to the worst, I could always go and sit on one of the narrow benches which lined the sports hall.

Eventually, as in most sports, because we unsporting boys *were* spoiling it for everybody else, we were quietly sidelined, passed over and then completely ignored. We were still forced to participate somehow, but we were invariably left out on the wing, as far back as possible, in the distant outfield, beyond the boundary. We were called defenders because we just might get in the way of somebody running toward goal with the ball. We might not know the first thing about cricket, but we could still catch a ball, surely? Even a solid, painful cricket ball hurtling toward you at a hundred miles an hour with everyone watching shouting, Catch It, Catch It. Surely we could still do that? Surely, *that* wasn't too much to ask?

I stood in mud up to my ankles waiting to catch a spinning rugby ball that never came my way, and for which I was grateful. I walked up and down the boundary of fifteen-a-side football teams making sure the ball was always moving in the opposite direction. I was told I had no team spirit and that this, later in life, in whatever job or profession I chose to follow, would be considered both a weakness and a failing.

One year, our P.E. master was a Sheffield-born Olympian, a tall, bronzed man with a crew-cut who, in addition to his teaching qualifications, brought both Olympic glory and an actual, official Olympic-issue starting pistol to the school. I came to despise the man. His whole life revolved around sport and exercise, self-improvement and self-acclaim. One term, he wrote, simply, 'Who?' on my report card. Hilarious. And something else for my father to afterwards endlessly repeat.

My father considered himself a sporting man, but watched all his sport on Saturday afternoon television. What was wrong with me? he wanted to know. Since moving to my new school, my mother had bought me a football shirt, boots, shorts, vests, everything, the lot, so why wasn't I at least making the effort? He challenged me to races, which I refused. He offered to give me a fifty-yard start in a hundred-yard race, rolling up his sleeves as he said it. I skulked away. He pretended to teach me how to box, prodding me in the chest and slapping me across the face with his fingers, telling me to punch him back, promising not to retaliate if I did this.

Once, in the club car park, when he was passing after parking his car, he joined in the game of French cricket – cricket for sissies – I was playing with some other boys. His turn to bowl, he said, taking the ball. An overhand lob that hit my shin. Out! Leg before wicket. L.B.W. He raised his arms, turning in a circle to acknowledge the sparse, nervous applause when it finally came. My tearful objection that the bowler was meant to bowl *underarm* in French cricket was met with derision from him. There I was again – making up the rules as I went along to suit myself, laying blame everywhere except where it belonged. What was I going to do next – run off crying to my mother? Who was batting next? Him, that's who. Come on, he didn't have all day.

35

THE unequalled and long-anticipated highlight of my every childhood year was our annual holiday to the East Yorkshire coast. More keenly anticipated by me than even Christmas, our week in a small, spartan chalet overlooking Thornwick Bay, north of the chalk cliffs of Flamborough Head, was a different world. My parents became different people for the duration of that one magical week, and few of the rules and constraints which governed our lives at home applied.

The holiday camp was called Sea Farm Camp, a three-word combination which said it all, and which I always appreciated seeing on the giant billboard at the camp's entrance as we drove in amid the swathes of grass, caravans and chalets.

To begin with, we stayed in buildings that might have been erected during the war, and which resembled the prefabs which still existed in great numbers back home in Sheffield. These simple buildings were raised on short brick columns and had wooden steps rising to the doorway.

Inside, there was a room containing a fold-down table, two gas rings, a sink and a cupboard, seating which folded out into a double bed, and gas mantles on the wall, which had to be coaxed carefully into life each night, and which filled the room with their hissing and the faint smell of gas as they burned.

This fuel was bought upon arrival at the camp office. The canisters were then dragged to a paving stone beside the chalet and connected by my father. A full canister lasted a week for lighting, heating and cooking. The dusty, popping heater filled the room with its own distinctive noise and aroma.

Beyond this room was a bedroom. There was no toilet or bathroom, but a short distance away, across a grassy slope, was a simple building in which four shower heads hung from the ceiling. And perhaps these were the greatest novelty of all to a family who had never before used a shower, and who knew of no one who possessed one in their own home. The water was never more than lukewarm, and none of us ever showered without wearing our underwear or swimming costume.

Later, when our preferred, and considerably cheaper, chalets were demolished, we moved across the camp to a more recently erected structure, clad in wood, with a pitched felt roof, and with double doors which opened on to a small, raised platform, where we could all sit and look out at the camp before us.

People sat in the sun, called to each other – invariably to ask where they were from – and drank tea out in the open. The sense of occasion was everywhere and in everything we did on those holidays.

In these larger holiday homes – still called chalets – there was a second bedroom, and occasionally my widowed Nan would come with us. Linoleum covered the floor – quickly dusted with pale sand – and small, faded rugs lay scattered over this. Holidaying women still did their housework each morning. Flocks of gulls gathered and screamed for any available food and landed noisily on the thin roof throughout the day and night.

In addition to the camp shop – daylight robbery, according to my mother; they wanted *how much* for a loaf of bread? – there was also a nearby farm where milk, eggs, bread and bacon could be bought. The milk came in cartons, not bottles, with the name of the farm on the side. The opening of these cartons was delegated to my father, who, each time he did this, expounded on the knack he possessed. We were all happy to believe that the eggs, bread and bacon were also produced at the farm, even though there was no evidence of this.

The chalet contained everything a holidaying family might need for a week's stay – bedding, towels, crockery and cutlery – and checking on all this – a list was fixed to a cupboard door – and cooking on the gas rings and making up the beds and laying the table was always a great pleasure to my mother. It was almost as though we were all playing at house, far removed from the routines and anxieties of our usual, actual, everyday existence back at home.

We woke to the sun, planned the day's events and outings, ate makeshift meals together, came and went to no fixed timetable. We stayed up late and played with other holidaying children of the same age. Even my parents indulged themselves in the relaxed routine, and occasionally returned with new friends or went with them to their own chalets and caravans.

At the heart of the camp stood the clubhouse, providing drink and entertainment every night of the week: trios of musicians, cabaret artists, comedians, singers and glamorous dancers, all of them performing throughout the evening, and all of it absolutely free.

It was my father's irresistible and inevitable boast that we would see musicians and singers in that clubhouse ten times better and more accomplished than anything – and he used the term advisedly – that had ever appeared on *Top of the Pops*. Musicians? Singers? Don't make him laugh.

Alongside the club was a television room in which the younger children were deposited and afterwards visited from time to time with bottles of pop and packets of crisps. The night was filled with children wandering the camp in the warm summer dark, scrambling beneath the raised chalets and caravans, sitting on the swings sharing cigarettes and following the thin, baked paths though the surrounding fields toward the cliff tops and coves. One of the biggest attractions was a sandpit into which a small, derelict fishing boat had been dragged and abandoned and in which we all imagined we were sailors or pirates out on the open sea.

Alongside the shop with its essentials, cheap plastic toys and comic postcards was a small amusement arcade, in which everything cost a penny to operate, and into whose machines we daily fed our carefully rationed holiday savings: a moving conveyer belt of black and white stripes along which coins were rolled and then fell, winning sixpence if they landed wholly in the white; a ball bearing flicked around a metal spiral into a row of waiting holes rising in value toward their centre. There were pinball tables, but to begin with these were beyond my understanding and control, and mostly dominated by older boys showing off to older girls. Brightly coloured miniature racehorses ran in a line and you laid a bet on the winner, the cheapest payouts usually winning by a good few lengths. There was a laughing policeman or sailor, as there was in all arcades, and other clockwork cabinets in which miniature rooms were filled with candles, wandering ghosts and flickering lights. Men had nooses put round their necks and were dropped through the trapdoors of miniature gallows.

Any winnings, briefly hoarded, endlessly counted and displayed, were invariably fed back into the slots of these simple but rewarding pleasures. We only had ourselves to blame when all our money was gone. But even here the reality of home was often suspended, and both my mother and father would search their purses and pockets for yet more loose change before sending us out again.

Even on the rare occasions when it rained, there was still pleasure to be had in the board games to be found in the chalet cupboard or borrowed from our new friends – something else we would never have considered doing back at home.

Surrounding the camp was open countryside leading to high chalk cliffs, small pebble-filled bays and the sea beyond. A cafe sat on the cliff top, opening early in the morning to sell mugs of tea and bacon sandwiches to keen anglers who gathered on the rocks below.

Few fish larger than half a pound were ever caught, and mostly all the bait was lost to scavenging crabs, overenthusiastic casting or the turbulence of the tide as it came and went amid the chalk arches and deep gullies.

At North Landing there was a small fishing fleet, and we gathered to watch the boats pulled into and out of the sea by ancient tractors. Crab and lobster pots were laid in the deeper water, and most of the houses on the road into Flamborough village advertised freshly caught and boiled seafood for sale. My mother bought steaming crabs and we sat around the chalet table retrieving the sparse meat with cocktail sticks. We gathered buckets of winkles from the rocks at low tide and my mother boiled these and we teased out the snail-like innards with pins. The chalet filled with the smell of all this and it permeated our clothes.

The highlight day of this highlight week was when my father and I went out together fishing in a rowing boat from Bridlington harbour. We were given hand lines and a biscuit tin filled with stinking mussels and pieces of fish. My father rowed us half a mile offshore and we sat for three or four hours fishing in the pale green water. The boats were unsteady and shallow, and their bottoms slowly filled with water as we waited. A second tin was provided to bale this out. My father was an efficient rower, and I imagined this was something else he had learned in the army, perhaps on the Suez Canal itself. There were ponds in most of the Sheffield parks, and men rowed their wives and girlfriends on these.

My father and I were never accompanied on these expeditions – neither my mother nor sister would ever have considered the trip and my brother was still too young. We sat together, tugging at our lines and calling out to the men in nearby boats. We all turned to watch each time a fish was caught.

Mostly we landed small plaice and dabs weighing only a few ounces, but all of which were kept and later handed over to my mother. Occasionally, we would catch an eel, a codling or a vigorous mackerel, and every tug on the line was a new excitement, both of us peering over the side for that first silvery flash of the fish beneath us. It was never an equal contest – the lead weight which held the line on the bottom frequently weighed more than the fish themselves, and the only real challenge came when two or more mackerel were caught simultaneously. They were the only fish which offered any real resistance to us, the challenge coming largely in the need to avoid catching our fingers on the barbed hooks as we attempted to shake the struggling fish free.

Men took out sandwiches and flasks and some even lugged crates of ale with them. They toasted each other across the open water. My father would insist he could see my mother, sister and brother amid the thousands of brightly coloured dots on the distant beach. People stood in the shallow water and waved at us and we waved back.

On one occasion, the sea became suddenly rough and the boat in which we sat started to rock uncontrollably. A launch came out from the harbour and a man with a loudhailer told the fishermen to start rowing back to the pier. He moved in a half circle around the scattered boats, herding them together like a dog rounding up sheep. Some boats ran aground on a sandbank and men climbed out and stood on this. We gathered closer and waited on the water for the squall to pass. Men complained of the paid-for time they had wasted, all those uncaught fish still swimming beneath us.

When we did finally return to the harbour, we made a show of carrying our plastic bags of small fish proudly along the Promenade in search of my mother. Our catch was wrapped in newspaper and deposited in the warm boot of the car. It was never anything less than disappointing to see the shiny, struggling fish we had earlier caught beheaded, gutted and filleted ready to be eaten.

There was a great deal of bone and fin and little actual flesh. We seldom ate fish at home except battered from the chip shop. My holiday mother floured and fried our catch, and my holiday father told us that it would taste all the better for having been caught by the two of us. It was another rare proud moment of my young life, even if copious amounts of salt, vinegar and tomato ketchup were needed to make what we had caught edible. Those fish we didn't eat, my father gave away to holidaymakers in the nearby chalets, always on the promise of a pint in the clubhouse later.

Most of everything else we ate on these holidays we took with us from home. My mother would build up these supplies throughout the year, setting aside endless tins for the occasion. Treats for the week included cans of steamed pudding which contained their own sweet sauces, and ready-made steak and kidney pies whose crusts rose golden and flaky in the small oven once the can lid was removed. Tinned milk supplemented that from the farm, and I preferred this, especially condensed milk, which could be spooned from the can like a sweet, creamy syrup.

The days toward the end of this near-miraculous week were tainted with the gathering sense of foreboding that everything was coming too soon to its end. We had to be out of the chalet by noon on Saturday, just as we had not been allowed to arrive before two. The building would be stripped, cleaned, checked and re-provisioned, and then another lucky, excited family with its own lucky, excited children would move in and take over where we had left off for another long year.

We drove into Bridlington or somewhere nearby and seldom left for home until later in the afternoon. My father wanted to avoid all the other departing holidaymakers and the traffic jams they would undoubtedly be causing. As a consequence, we arrived back in Sheffield late at night or in the early hours of the following morning.

Usually on this return journey we would stop off at one or two roadhouses so that my mother and father could go in for a drink. When we arrived home my brother and sister would have to be carried from the car to their beds and I would go to mine. My mother would put the kettle on and my father would announce that we were leaving the unloading of the car until the following morning, as though he too hoped to prolong the pleasure of what had just so abruptly ended, and to which nothing else in our annual routine would come even close until the following year's identical week.

36

H AVING stopped me from taking early morning papers, my father then insisted I found another job – this time preferably one which in no way interrupted his own daily timetable. I was fifteen. He told me again that I needed to grow up and to stop behaving as though the world owed me a living. It was time for me to start paying my way in that world. There were lessons I needed to learn, he said, important lessons; and lessons I needed to learn sooner rather than later: lessons, I had long since understood, in what it was like to have been him.

A boy at school told me there were jobs available stacking shelves at a nearby supermarket. Fine Fare, a forerunner of later, larger supermarkets, employed two dozen locals, half of whom were schoolboys and girls, taken on primarily to unload the twice-weekly deliveries of goods and then to wheel these out and stack them on the waiting shelves. The store was open six days a week, and until nine in the evening two days a week. Deliveries came throughout the day, with major loads on Thursday and Saturday. Accordingly, most of the boys worked all day Saturday, Sundays when called upon, and two or three evenings immediately after school during the week.

I walked to the store from school, kept a change of clothes there to protect my hire-purchase uniform, and worked until nine, when I continued my journey home. My homework suffered because of this routine, but I managed to keep up with this.

It was of no concern to my father that this new work might interrupt my schoolwork. It was more important, he insisted, that I was now able to start paying for my board. My mother, naturally, refused to take even this token payment. I started earning three times what delivering papers had brought me, and the money came with an actual payslip, deductions already deducted.

When we were asked to work on Sundays the pay was doubled. This often involved trips to distant, unfamiliar stores to undertake stock-taking while the shop was closed.

I worked with a dozen other regular boys, alongside the under-managers and the women and girls who sat at the checkouts. A kind of democracy existed in the storeroom and easy, popular jobs were always fairly combined with the harder, dirtier work.

Unloading the delivery lorries was always popular, operating the tailgate lifts and rolling the stacked pallets back and forth while the drivers sat in their cabs and smoked, coming out only when everything was unloaded to tally the pallets against their dockets and then sending one of us to fetch an under-manager to sign for the delivery. These men asked us if we'd checked each load, and though we hadn't, we said we had. Invoices were signed and the pallets were rolled into the storeroom and then out on to the shop floor, where everything was transferred to the shelves.

The least popular job in the store was working the baler in the windowless baling room, where empty cardboard boxes were flattened and then bound into bundles ready for collection. A giant press was manually wound down on the stacked cardboard and this was compressed into bales, which were then bound with oily wire. The door was unbolted and the heavy bales manhandled out of the small room into the yard behind the store. Newcomers were tested in the baling room. Dragging the bales outside was the hardest work of all, and I saw smaller boys cry with the effort and their sense of failure. Men from the butchery department often came out to help anyone who was struggling. They called the under-managers bastards for making us do the work, telling us that they, the butchers, were Union men and that we weren't. None of us understood them.

Saturday mornings at the store always began with price alterations. We were given lists of the products to be changed, gathered these off the shelves and then took them out of sight of the customers to alter them. In the early days, the tinned goods were ink-stamped and we erased this with a solvent called acetone which we were told to avoid breathing in as we worked. Pricing guns which printed paper labels arrived soon afterwards and deprived us of the small pleasure of sniffing in the acetone.

The Fine Fare chain, the manager told us, prided itself on being at the cutting edge of retail technology and practice. We were told to start referring to the store as a hypermarket, the first in Sheffield. Disappointingly, all this involved was tipping boxes of unstamped tins into giant wire baskets, where they lay in untidy mounds waiting to be bought.

Everything in the store was orange and white, including the uniforms and caps of the women workers. In the storeroom we wore long soiled aprons similar to the one I wore at school for my woodwork lessons.

Whole carcases of beef, lamb and pork were delivered to the butchery department, and the men there carved these up and displayed them in shrink-wrapped polystyrene cartons. I admired the skill of these men with their slender knives, and for a long time I knew that when I left school without whatever qualifications I was expected to gain, then becoming a butcher – hopefully in that very store – would not be a disappointing occupation.

The men carried the carcases from the refrigerated lorries and worked swiftly, deftly and meticulously, chopping, slicing and carving to ensure that nothing went to waste. Ears, noses and cheeks were carved out, packaged, weighed, priced and displayed. Liver, kidneys, tripe; cow heels, chitling, bag. Pigs' tails were sold to thicken stews, lambs' tongues to be pressed. Pieces of meat and fat that might otherwise be wasted were bagged and sold as pet food, largely in the knowledge that this was not where the bags of scraps would end up.

The butchers wore caps to hold in their hair, and white jackets and trousers stained with blood. They congregated with us in the rear yard to smoke and to discuss the women who worked on the checkouts.

Over the fridges outside the butchery department hung two-way mirrors, revealing the food in the cabinets below. When a woman was forced to lean over the cabinets to reach something low down or toward the rear of the display, the butchers would call each other to gather and look. The boys, too, were included in this and we stood with the men and repeated their lascivious remarks. They laughed with us and at us, and we appreciated both. They sent us out to ask the women what they wanted and then for them to wait while we fetched it. The women studied their hairdos and their make-up in the mirrors while they waited, pouting at the invisible men beyond.

At dinnertime we shared our meals in a small canteen. The store employed a cook, who created meals from damaged cans, less-than-fresh vegetables and out-of-date stock. As we ate, we practised flirting with the girls training at the checkouts and they told us about the actual, real life, flesh and blood boyfriends they already had. The older women gave us cigarettes, and they too made disparaging remarks about the under-managers. Every time one of the men came into the room he was assailed by their remarks. It was all done in good humour, but the men, like the rest of us, were never allowed to forget their place in the unofficial hierarchy of the store, where workers were always workers, management always management.

On Thursday nights, following a delivery and then the closure of the store, the manager went home and the under-managers visited nearby pubs. The rest of us, having been told what needed to be achieved before our own departure, roamed the empty store stealing food and drink. A solitary television camera pointed at the drinks and tobacco kiosk and we knew to avoid this. If the under-managers suspected anything, then they were always careful not to reveal their own unofficial absences from the store.

As a perk, we were allowed to buy dented and damaged cans at a reduced price to take home. I dented cans of that still-precious salmon and ham, marked them down and then sold these at a small profit to my mother, who was always happy at the saving. She told me what to look out for and to seize for her.

Unlike her husband, my mother was scrupulously honest, and if I experienced any guilt at what I was doing, then it was not because I was stealing money from her, but because she was now implicated in my own dishonesty. On the few occasions she asked me to keep an eye out for something more specific, I stole to order and felt even worse. She would never have condoned my crimes and would have been distraught if she'd known what I was doing.

On one occasion, I packed up a few pounds of expensive cooked meats, sealed this in a bag and marked it up as pet food. I gave this to my mother when she came into the store, telling her it was for our Jack Russell. Upon my return home, she discovered what I had done and refused to use the meat on sandwiches. It would have lasted the five of us for a week in our lunch boxes. Instead, she insisted on feeding the meat to the dog. I tried to repay the money she had given me, but she insisted I keep it. She guessed then what had been happening with all the dented tins of salmon and ham and afterwards refused to accept anything more from me.

Whatever remorse I might have felt at both alarming and then disappointing my mother like this did nothing to temper my actual thieving. Everything I stole from then onward, I sold elsewhere. She told me not to tell my father of any of this, knowing that he would have encouraged me to continue taking the food home, telling her that she was being ridiculous and costing them money. Besides, he would tell her, I was only doing what *anyone* in my position would have done. I was showing a bit of initiative at last. And it was only this – this understanding that I was becoming formed more in the mould of the man rather than that of my honest, fearful, careful mother – which finally gave me cause to guiltily consider all that I was doing and, perhaps, becoming.

37

I N addition to the ever-present Freemans catalogue, from which we bought our everyday clothes, our outfits for best, our soft furnishings, some of our household goods and birthday and Christmas presents, my mother also became an agent for Avon – an Avon Lady: *Ding Dong, Avon Calling* – selling perfumes, cosmetics and cut-above toiletries.

My mother visited neighbours and relatives with the glossy catalogues. There was very little commission to be made from the Freemans sales – the advantage of running it coming from the small personal discount she was given, being able to make affordable weekly payments, and thereafter, as with most credit, to extend these payments endlessly into the future. There was always an understanding that running the catalogues was a worthwhile thing for her to do because she was offering similar advantages to women living in circumstances identical to her own.

The Avon catalogue, on the other hand, suggested luxury, displaying things that were seldom entirely necessary, but whose purchase would always say something about the women being tempted by them, and who had then chosen and bought them. Avon offered a larger commission to my mother, but all too often this also came in the form of reduced-price and, allegedly, free Avon goods. My mother never complained that this was unfair of the company, and instead used her commission to provide herself with those birthday and Christmas presents which everyone seemed to appreciate.

Monthly repayments to Avon, like those to the Co-op for my school uniform, were always considered to exist at a higher level than the tick or never-never repayments taken on elsewhere. There was at least some degree of respectability attached to both the Freemans and Avon repayments. After all, nothing in the Freemans catalogue was exactly shoddy or cheaper than elsewhere. And some of the goods on offer in the Avon brochure were genuinely luxurious and might have been coveted by anybody – goods such as the rose-shaped and scented soaps on a rope or the dolphin-shaped bottles of blue bubble bath to families who otherwise washed their children at the kitchen sink and who used washing-up liquid as shampoo.

I admired and appreciated the various moulded soaps my mother ordered, and I seldom used my own gifts to actually wash with, preferring to keep them as a sort of ornament. Avon provided my mother with miniature samples of most of what they sold, along with gift cards and special presentation bags, all of which added to the high-end appeal of the purchases, and which my mother appreciated more than most.

It was understood – and certainly by my mother – that many of those neighbours, friends and workmates to whom she sold these products didn't necessarily want or need them, but that they were buying them from her to support her in her endeavours to boost her own low income and quickly spent wages. They were women like her, all of them in careful control of small, stretched and uncertain household budgets, and so they understood perfectly the true and exact nature of the transactions they were undertaking. All the same, the catalogues were a rare means of escape for my mother. They got her out of the house, they gave her an interest beyond her home and family, and they bought in a bit of extra income, even if sometimes it wasn't in the form of actual cash. Dealing with the orders and the collected payments gave my mother authority and responsibility: it put her in charge of things; it made her a responsible figure in the lives of women who actually appreciated her efforts on their behalves. The catalogues became her domain, nothing whatsoever to do with my father.

My mother once told me that women like her would always buy from the Avon brochure simply because they no longer felt comfortable or confident buying those same products from the beautifully dressed and perfectly made-up saleswomen in the city centre's many department stores. My mother's customers were women who were no longer young, and who, like her, had lost their figures to child-bearing and to the physical drudgery of their everyday lives – women who were now reluctant to approach those beaming salesgirls at their shining counters and ask their advice. My mother, on the other hand, was the perfect person to ask. Women confided in her, asked her opinion; it was another part of the work's appeal for her.

The gifts my mother was occasionally awarded by Avon were proudly shown to our few visitors. The same probably happened in all those other households, where neither a dolphin-shaped bottle nor blue, scented bubble bath was an everyday thing.

The only disadvantage to all of this were the rare occasions when my mother tallied up her takings prior to sending off a money order and found herself a few shillings or even pounds short. She invariably made this up herself and then went in search of the missing or miscalculated money. The exact amount was always made up to accompany the catalogue orders. On some occasions, when the shortfall was a large one, she wept at the further financial juggling she would now be forced to undertake to ensure everything was accounted for. Often, other jars and cans secreted around the house would be raided to ensure the correct amounts were made up. No one in that wider, watching world was going to point a finger at her, and especially not when her good name and reputation for honesty and reliability were concerned. The small dark clouds of debt forever floated over that household and everyone within it was aware of these.

38

O NCE every four or five years, we took an uncharacteristic risk and abandoned our usual holiday on the Yorkshire coast for one considerably less familiar and, occasionally, further afield. The excited anticipation of the holiday remained, but it was a different kind of anticipation – one now tinged with uncertainty, and with the possibility that not everything might be favourably compared to the previous year's holiday, and the one before that, and the one before that. It seemed to me that we lived already with sufficient risk and uncertainty in our every-day lives to be taking any chance whatsoever with something as precious – something as *vital* – to us as our annual holiday.

One year we went to a self-catering flat in Whitby. Three rooms in a house overlooking the harbour, a cooker which ran on Calor gas canisters, and whose windowsills and doorstep were caked with an inch of seagull droppings. It was a change, but not a welcome one. The gas canisters were a reassuring bonus, but I still preferred a caravan or chalet – the *proper* home for a holiday.

My main memory of the holiday is of catching crabs the size of a penny along the high harbour walls, keeping these in a plastic carton and expecting them to be admired by every passer-by.

There was another flat in Llandudno – our only ever foreign holiday, my father joked – about which I can remember nothing.

A caravan holiday in Skegness was nearer the mark. A vast field of perfectly manicured lawn laid out with row after row of thousands of near-identical caravans, white, cream, pale blue and yellowish – seaside colours – some with canvas awnings and small balconies for a touch of luxury. Beds, seats and tables came out of and went back into those familiar and much-appreciated recesses according to when they were required.

Pale, soft grass-topped dunes and then the calm, shallow sea half a mile distant. At the centre of the camp was a small funfair, free to paying visitors and an unimaginable bonus to parents with small, easily excitable children.

The one very memorable and almost – to me at least – unbelievable event during that solitary holiday in Skegness was when my mother took me, and me alone, her eldest son, up in an aeroplane. There was a small airfield close to the caravan park, and short airborne excursions were advertised in the canopies of the flimsy-looking aircraft parked along the grass runway.

My mother and I were the only passengers. Cold air rushed through the rattling windows. My mother sat beside the pilot and I sat between them. The small plane took off, twisted and banked, and the fields of caravans beneath us suddenly revealed themselves to us in all their unsuspected patterns. The lines of the camps and farmland and beach and shoreline drifted left to right and then right to left of us every time we turned.

The flight lasted only ten or twenty minutes, and we soon came down to earth, stopping quickly and quietly once the wheels were again back on the grass. The pleasure and excitement of that one short flight was beyond all comparison in my young life. All I knew of planes and pilots and flying I knew from war films and my models and my growing collection of Commando comic books. For those all-too-short minutes I had been part of that life.

Skegness, Ingoldmells, Mablethorpe, all identical, all devoted to the crowds of holidaying miners and steelworkers and factory hands, and all enjoyed with a pleasure so intense that it was perhaps fortunate that the holidays lasted no longer than a week. We did occasionally hear of people who had actually *flown* to their holiday destinations, and who had then spent a fortnight there, but not us.

39

WHEN I was fifteen, an age when I was at least able to begin to understand the true nature of the lives being lived around me, and when I finally started to see my father for what he truly was, he started picking up a woman who lived further up the street, and giving her a lift to work each morning.

Day after day, my mother stood at the front window net curtains and peered out as he reversed his car along the road to wait outside the woman's house. They argued over this. He insisted he was simply giving the woman a lift, that it was no trouble to him, that she worked somewhere along his route, that it was a friendly gesture, that he was being neighbourly. It was in his nature, he insisted. Wasn't he even allowed to carry out this one small act of kindness without being scrutinized and condemned? *Jesus Christ Almighty*, what did she want of him, what did she expect? The arguments penetrated every one of our thin walls and echoed around every small room.

We all, in our own way, understood that what was happening was considerably more than an act of neighbourly kindness. It had never been in my father's nature to be either of those things. My mother called the woman his fancy piece. It was the height of condemnation. I don't ever remember seeing my father and the woman together, even sitting side by side in his precious car, and I have no memory of what she looked like or who she might have been. She deserved her title, it seemed to me then, solely on the grounds that she herself must certainly have known who my father was and what family he had living so close to her own home. Even living a street away would have made a difference to all this terrible reckoning.

My mother stood at the net curtains and told me to go away. It was nothing, she said, keeping her face from me. She was just looking out at the weather, seeing what she needed to wear for her own short journey to work. My father left the house at ten past eight, the rest of us ten minutes later. Our separate timetables were carefully calculated and stretched to their limits; it was always a fraught ten minutes in that small house.

We would all avoid my mother as she stood at the window and had her worst fears confirmed – that everything in her shrunken, proscribed and regimented life – her home, her husband, her children, her job, her means of support, her standing in the world, the regard of her own and other families – was now in jeopardy: fears worse and more all-consuming than any of the rest of us could even begin to understand. She waited at the window in her dressing gown, ungirdled, her face without make-up, her body, arms and legs hanging heavily on her, and watched my father in his car with this other woman. Perhaps she even knew who the woman was; she would certainly have known *something* of her, living so close; perhaps it added the insult to the injury of my father's insistence that he was only being neighbourly.

I got it into my head that the woman was younger, slimmer and more glamorous than my mother. As glamorous as *she* had once been, perhaps, but was no longer. I imagined this woman as one of those women coming out of the club on a Saturday night, a woman in a fake leopard-skin coat, her peroxide hair piled high on her head. She was a common enough figure, this woman. We all knew the type. And I knew she was precisely the type who would appeal to my father and all his vanities – a man who needed his every remark and action to be praised, endorsed and commented upon. He was easily flattered, easily persuaded. He was still able to convince himself that no one knew he was wearing a wig, that it contributed to his youth, attraction and virility. He continued to spend a large part of his life with other men who were exactly like him; they were a self-sustaining tribe.

Nice aftershave, a snazzy tie, a bit of the old tomfoolery, a few nicker in his sky rocket. A man who knew how to look after himself – and it showed – a proper gent, drove his own motor; whatever you wanted, he'd do his best, never paid over the odds for anything in his life, half the asking price at most, usually less. Always one of those men who knew a man who knew another man. And he knew how to treat people properly, always stood his round – ask anyone.

I imagined it all – everything he might appear to be to this other woman – and I felt aggrieved for my mother.

It occurred to me at the time to wonder how much of all this my younger sister and brother truly understood, and how much I might reveal to them if they asked me about our mother's behaviour, her tears and her shaking as she stood in her dressing gown at the window. It was certainly something none of us could ignore. Did they even know what a fancy woman or a flighty piece was? Did I, for that matter? The worst I could actually imagine was my father, in his car, dressed smartly for work, his briefcase with its flask and sandwiches on the seat behind him, sitting there with the woman close beside him. I couldn't even imagine him kissing her. Any affection he ever displayed to us, his family, was always done for a reason – cajoling, ameliorating – and I doubted if I understood the true meaning of the word anyway. I certainly couldn't imagine anything else happening within the confines of that car.

I imagined the woman laughing at what he said, blowing the smoke of her cigarette out of the side of her mouth through an inch of open window; I saw him lighting two cigarettes in his own mouth and then handing one to her, a common enough gesture. It was an intimacy of sorts – the only sort I understood between the adults I knew.

And because this was *all* I could imagine, I also imagined that my mother, in her usual melodramatic fashion, was making considerably more of the situation than it warranted. Perhaps it *was* just a friendly gesture, a kindness even, some-thing that might save the woman a few shillings each week when my father had three empty car seats going begging. In fact, I considered his greatest betrayal of my mother – of all of us, for that matter – to be connected to the car: here was a complete stranger getting a lift every single day, and at her own convenience, when the rest of us were driven somewhere or other only four or five times a year at the most.

I certainly didn't understand any of my mother's greater fears, of what this picking up of his fancy woman might actually lead to. My mother accused him of seeing the woman at other times. In fact, she wouldn't be surprised if my father didn't arrange to meet her at one or other of his pubs. He told her that, as usual, she was being ridiculous, over-reacting, showing him up and once again making a fool of herself. All she saw, he shouted at her, was what she wanted to see. Besides, who was *she* to tell *him* what to do and what not to do?

If she wanted to be looking for blame, then why didn't she start with herself? What did she expect of him? He was only human, only flesh and blood. These arguments – all arguments – ended with him leaving the house, slamming every door behind him and then driving off. Leaving my mother crying where she sat and saying that she hoped he was driving carefully, that by rights he shouldn't even be driving in that state. Whenever she said this to him on his way out of the house he laughed at her and told her to think about *why* he was in that state and whose fault it would be, who would be to blame, if he *did* have an accident. That's right – *hers*. She hadn't thought of that, had she? No, well, think on. At least with him gone from the house she'd have time to think about what she'd said and done, what she'd accused him of, and then consider the error of her ways. We all would.

I doubt if this picking up of the woman lasted for very long. And I don't know what – if anything of any consequence – actually happened between them.

My father was right – my mother *was* prone to melodramatic exaggeration and self-pity, and both became more prominent as she got older, even as she felt his grip on her slowly weaken. She might once have believed that all boyfriends and then husbands were like my father – just as *I* had once believed all fathers were much the same – but that gradually changed as they grew older together, as he became considerably more dependent on her, and as their own children and wider families slowly withdrew from them.

40

F ROM the Saint Cuthbert's Cubs, I graduated at twelve or thirteen to the Saint Cuthbert's Scout Troop, and was immediately disappointed by the change. In the Cubs we had all been much the same age, but in the Scouts there were boys from twelve to eighteen, and the whole organization was run on a more hierarchical and militaristic basis.

There was no leader's wife to mother us. We were ordered rather than told what to do, how to behave, and every misdemeanour in our behaviour, response or even dress was pointed out to everyone else present at our weekly gatherings.

The basic rituals of these meetings remained much the same, but I quickly understood that too much about the Scouts was connected to growing up and playing a part in the world rather than indulging in childhood fantasies of rural escape and survival in the wild. It was the same church hall, the same small patch of grass, but, essentially, everything was different, and either disappointing or even vaguely threatening to me.

There were more weekends away in vast fields or woodlands on the outskirts of the city. We were encouraged to mix with the youths of other troops and, sometimes, with the blue-clad Girl Guides who occasionally attended these gatherings.

I started again on my badge collecting, but soon discovered that attaining these now – receiving them following a small payment at a regular monthly ceremony – was considerably more difficult than in the Cubs, where everyone had been more or less rewarded for everything they had undertaken. More rigid systems of scoring operated in the Scouts, and failure was commonplace, followed immediately by starting again. Failure, we were told, was part of life, something everyone must experience. However unhappy our failures might make us, they were at least character-building – but only if the boys accepted those failures in the right frame of mind.

Everyone in the Scouts was made to play a band instrument, usually a drum or a bugle, and because I was unmusical, I chose the latter, reasoning that I could march amid twenty or thirty other buglers and merely pretend to be blowing. I puffed out my cheeks and then let the air wander feebly out through the polished metal coil. I marched and looked the part. The bugle was decorated with silky green and golden cords and at least these loops and tassels swung and swayed in time with the instruments all around me.

I came to dread the Sunday morning church parades, when we formed up on the quiet streets of late-sleepers and then blasted into life without warning as the bass drum player set both the tempo of the music and the pace of our marching. Scouts carrying embroidered banners, their own golden tassels swaying with the motion, marched ahead of us, the weight of the heavy tapestries and their poles and ropes supported by leather harnesses strapped firmly to the chests of the boys chosen as flag bearers. It was an honour to be chosen to carry the banners, and one that needed to be earned. More character-building.

After a year, the younger Scouts graduated from short trousers to long – just as at school – and then shortly after that the whole uniform changed – a different shirt and a beret instead of a cap. I became even more detached from the pleasure I had once gained from belonging to the troop.

One weekend we were taken to a camp at Thorpe Hesley, where an assault course built of logs and cables was the alleged highlight of the gathering. I climbed a sloping telegraph pole to the top of a ten-foot-high stockade and was then instructed to jump on to the padded matting below. I did this, landed badly – presumably because I hadn't been listening to the man telling me how to jump safely and land well – and sprained my ankle, unable afterwards to put any weight on my foot.

Youths coming after me jumped, rolled as instructed, leapt to their feet and ran off laughing excitedly along the course. I sat where I had landed, trying unsuccessfully not to cry at the pain I was now experiencing. My ankle was examined and bandaged. No real harm done, and certainly nothing to be allowed to get in the way of the fun everyone else was having. I was given a crutch to help me walk, allowing me to feign an agony I did not feel, and to briefly become the centre of everyone's attention. I limped hard over the next few days and was unable to attend the Scout meeting the following Friday night. And then the one after that. A fortnight later, I simply stopped attending. Perhaps someone from the organization or the church tried to contact my parents to find out why this had happened, or perhaps not. Or perhaps, as in my own mind, there was simply an understanding that I was not suited to the rigours and expectations of the organization, and that both it and I would benefit from our separation.

41

U NTIL the late sixties, neither of my parents possessed a
 bank account. Both brought home their wages either in
brown envelopes with a cellophane window or in self-sealing
opaque packets which were always ceremoniously held up
to the light and examined before being opened. The packets
held folded notes, ones and fives, a scatter of silver and copper,
and a payslip. These, too, were scrutinized, and all the unfair
deductions commented on: Income Tax, National Insurance,
Pension Contributions, Workplace Deductions, extra taxation
that no one saw coming. Very occasionally, there was an equally
unexpected rebate and this was always a cause for celebration.
The household budget was forever too finely tuned for all these
sums and figures *not* to be closely scrutinized.

My father's money was transferred directly to his wallet,
from which a small sum of housekeeping was then ceremoniously given to my mother as though it were a gift. This was
intended to pay for everything that he himself didn't require
for either his drinking or the running of his car.

My mother, upon receiving her own considerably smaller
wage, would tip the coins into her purse – copper one side,
silver the other – and then count out the notes and allocate
each of these its weekly or monthly purpose.

Money was slid into pay-books, into her catalogue kitties, into tins and jam jars for all the regular household bills and outgoings. Shillings and sixpences were piled in columns on top of the gas and electricity meters. A second purse at the back of a drawer took in the small weekly payments demanded by a Christmas club; a mug in the kitchen cupboard slowly filled, awaiting its own small emergency.

My father poured his own loose change into a drawer in a table in our little-used front room, and this, he boasted, often amounted to twenty or thirty pounds over the course of the year, something to buttress him against the additional expense of Christmas and his own extended holiday celebrations. All three of his children stole from this hidden hoard, a few of the coins each morning on our way out to school, only rarely replacing the smallest part of what we took. One year, my mother came to me in a panic a week before Christmas and made me confess my thieving. Aware of my father's reaction when he discovered his loss, she emptied several of her own savings books and jars and took the money to the bank at the bottom of the road to be converted into coins, which she scattered into the drawer in the hope that it would be enough. Following this, and aware of how close we had all come to another ruined, calamitous Christmas – an unthinkable event in a household where so little was actually looked forward to with any degree of genuine pleasure – our thieving mostly stopped.

When I was older, I regularly took a pound note from my father's payday wallet to fund my own early drinking forays, always careful to select the exact note and to leave everything as I'd found it on the bedroom dressing table. When each of the notes was new and crisp I was careful to take one from the end of the wad so that there was no break in the serial numbers. I checked the position and alignment of the wallet and looked carefully for any indication that my father, aware of what I was doing, had set a trap for me.

Neither of my parents ever owned a credit card. Credit – debt, really: H.P., tick, the never-never – was still a derogatory and demeaning word. A family member's new settee or cooker or carpet or sideboard might be admired, commented upon, envied in their presence, but was then afterwards dismissed as having been bought on the never-never. In that world, you only properly owned a thing when you had finished paying for it.

It was inconceivable to my parents that anything bought on credit – the honourable exception of my school uniform aside – could possibly be replaced before it had been fully paid for and then several more years had passed.

When I was fourteen or fifteen, things changed. My parents opened a bank account and each possessed a cheque book, something to be shown off and then hidden away and kept secure. My mother still made her weekly or monthly journeys to those offices and shops where she paid our regular bills, but now she did it with a cheque instead of the usual put-aside notes and coins. She practised her signature, a slow and precise piece of work with no hint of any flourish. It seemed a great step forward for a family obsessed with the comings and goings of money, to be able to actually spend it simply by filling in a blank cheque and then adding your name to it.

The other immediate advantage of the bank account was that you could write a cheque made payable to cash, present it to the teller in the bank and be immediately given money, usually in the form of those new, unused notes. Most transactions required some form of identification, and in the absence of a passport or, in my mother's case, a driving licence, a bill addressed to the householder was always deemed sufficient.

A branch of the bank – *our* bank – opened at the bottom of the road in a building resembling a small temple.

An additional benefit of withdrawing cash from the bank was that the customer could specify denominations. Small plastic bags, much coveted by all children, could now be obtained filled with brand new shilling pieces.

Possessing a bank account elevated the owner of that account. Banks stood as guarantors for people, stood surety. Bank managers were sought out to provide references for their customers. Having a bank account and using *this* to buy something on hire purchase was not the same as borrowing money without that account behind the transaction. We received Christmas cards from the bank, and cards from grateful customers were displayed at the tellers' windows each year.

On the occasions I accompanied my mother into the bank, I was always keen to see past the glass and the grilles and to look into the room beyond to see the giant metal safe sitting there. I knew well enough from the television that the safes – whole strongrooms in fact – existed, but I had never before seen one. And there it really was. A safe filled with thousands and thousands of pounds stacked in neat, bound bundles.

Bank robberies, thefts and burglaries were reported every day in the *Sheffield Star*, and having this building so close to where we lived brought the possibility of something similar happening here. When I went out with my friends with our guy to collect money in the weeks leading up to Bonfire Night, setting up on the steps of the bank seemed the most natural thing to do, as though the money inside might act as a magnet to money passing by outside. I was also aware that there were

Bank Holidays, and that the banks themselves closed early every afternoon so that the women inside could count up all the money they'd taken in during the short day's trading, presumably to bundle it up in wrappers and stack it inside the safe for the night.

A printed statement arrived in the post each month and was as closely scrutinized as the wage slips had once been, though these too continued to arrive in their clear envelopes, but now without any actual money attached. What my mother feared most was going overdrawn, inadvertently spending the bank's money and not our own. The tins and jars secreted around the house continued to be filled and emptied, and there remained that constant vigil over the precarious financial balance of our lives.

Cheque books arrived equally regularly through the post, and my mother invariably felt the need to explain to us that just because we now possessed twenty empty cheques, it did not mean that we possessed the money with which to fill and cash those cheques. It might have been a step up, a step in the right direction, but the ground beneath our feet, it seemed, was still the same uneven, shaky ground upon which we had always walked.

42

M Y father's cars were a source of great pride to him. Not so much the makes or models he owned – all were second-hand, and most were already old-fashioned-looking by the time he acquired them – but merely the fact that he owned the vehicles and all this implied on a street where there were perhaps only half a dozen other drivers.

Few of our neighbours owned cars, and so parking directly outside our own house was rarely a problem. Only when the club was featuring a special entertainer did parking become an issue for my father. Often, before leaving the house on one of his pub rounds, he would tell my mother to stay awake, to wait until the club emptied, and then to go outside and stand at *our* kerb to ensure no one else had the audacity to take the space before his return. His anger when he was forced to park even ten or twenty yards away made itself known to us through floors and walls.

He would wait, and upon hearing the interloper finally depart he would go back out and drive the short distance to this sacred space, often making a point of edging to within inches of the other strange cars parked on either side of him. Men from the club came drunkenly knocking to find out who owned what cars. He would deny all knowledge, his victory over these inconsiderate bastards confirmed and complete. Often, these strangers' cars would still be there the following morning awaiting collection later, making his small victory even sweeter to him.

Like all men, and despite his occupation in a garage, he undertook all repairs and servicing of the cars himself. Engines were invariably oil- and dirt-encrusted, and most car owners knew how to dismantle and clean these – briefly revealing their shining silver innards – and then return everything to its proper place. Cars were jacked up, supported on bricks, and wheels, brakes and gearboxes removed and examined. Parts were sandpapered, greased, filed, soldered, replaced and then everything was put confidently back together.

Bodywork and chrome trimmings were regularly washed, waxed and polished. It was easy to please my father by undertaking these laborious tasks, and he would make a point of inspecting all work before handing over any small payment.

My mother never learned to drive – none of the women in the family drove – and the use of the car for family excursions was restricted to our annual holiday and the odd day out during the long summer holidays. Mostly, the car was to get my father to and from work, and then, after work, to and from his various pubs.

I remember an Austin A40, a large, rounded cream-coloured car with bulbous wheel arches front and back and a running board which stretched between them. After this came a Singer Vogue followed by a two-tone Hillman Minx. The latter was mint- and emerald-green. All my father's cars seemed too large and cumbersome when set against the newer models – the Cortinas, Zodiacs and Zephyrs – whose very names contributed to their modernity and appeal.

All the cars we owned had leather upholstery, large, solid steering wheels, and carpet on the floor. In some, there were no flashing indicators, but rather illuminated plastic arms which rose from the window frames to point left or right.

All these steel-heavy cars rusted quickly and unstoppably in Sheffield's wet climate, and the holes and frayed metal edges on the bonnet or doors were constantly searched for, sanded down, filled, sanded again, buffed, undercoated, buffed again, painted and then waxed and polished as each defect appeared. Real men took a pride in such things. In addition to the rain and snow, the Sheffield air was filled with every kind of industrial and domestic smoke. None of it helped.

It was claimed by my father that a man who didn't know how to keep his car running and up to the mark didn't deserve to have one. It seemed a strange remark to make for a man who made his living repairing other people's cars.

Often, in our frequent lay-by stops to and from our annual holiday, he would gather with other drivers around their raised bonnets watching steam rise from overheated radiators, watching hot water drip from ruptured hoses, listening to strange knocking sounds, offering refills of oil and water, unscrewing hot caps with rag-wrapped hands, discussing various remedies.

One vivid memory is of him helping a stranded motorist in one such lay-by, who came to where we children waited with our mother and who then gave us each a ten-shilling note, thereby doubling what we had already saved to spend on our week away. The man told us that our father had solved a problem for him, allowing him to continue on his own journey, but that he had then refused to accept anything for his expertise and labour. The language, and the man's kind gesture, made the makeshift repair a great achievement, and I recall feeling proud of my father. Here was a well-spoken man with a car considerably better and newer than our own, and yet he had been unable to do for himself what my father had been able to undertake in a matter of minutes.

Before each of these annual long journeys – a hundred miles or more driven in five or six hours on narrow roads along convoluted, and occasionally unknown, routes – the engine was examined and everything topped up and the tyres inflated with a foot pump. My father even calculated the effect of the weight and distribution of our luggage on the pressures. It might not be much, but every mile driven on an under- or over-inflated tyre cost money, and only a complete and total mug paid out for no good reason.

43

THE Pole was a walker. A bulky, dark, middle-aged man forever fastened tight inside a dirty, belted raincoat. He walked from the top of the street to the bottom, where he stood for a few minutes before turning and walking back to the top, pausing every few steps on this uphill journey to rest against the low walls, draw on his cigarette, spit copiously and catch his breath. In addition to smoking, the man seemed always to be eating – slices of bread or pieces of chocolate, thinner slices of ham and cheese from the corner shop. Eating with his stained fingers, forever wiping his lips with his hand. I was well versed in the etiquette of eating, and the slobbering, crumb-dropping Pole broke every rule.

We waited for the man to pass by and then walked alongside him, calling him names and swearing at him, encouraging his incomprehensible outbursts of anger, and secure in the knowledge that he didn't understand a word we were saying. More than this – we also knew he would never threaten to tell our parents what we were doing, that his only aim was to get beyond us and to continue his endless, seemingly pointless walking.

When I remarked on the man to my mother, she told me to leave him alone. Something about the war. He was a Pole, she said, and though this meant nothing to me, it at least gave me his name. The Pole would shake his fist at us and shout at us in his own ridiculous language. Knowing that he possessed neither the breath nor the energy to chase us beyond a few steps only added to our amusement and to the pleasure of our taunting.

The man was short and squat, egg-shaped, his every bulge revealed by the tight raincoat. His head was spherical, his black hair shaved short and most of his face covered in heavy stubble. His thick eyebrows shielded his eyes and gave him an air of menace. His lips, too, were fat and pale and he blew small bubbles when he shouted at us. All cigarette smoke smelled, but the particular stink of his own filled the air long after he had gone. None of us knew where he lived, only that our road formed part of a circuitous walking route which never varied. There was something both pathetic and threatening about the man. There were tales of the boys he had grabbed out at and actually caught, and if we got too close to him then we too ran the risk of this happening to us. When my mother told me that the man might only have been trying to communicate with us in his own language, I knew she was wrong and that she was making excuses for him.

We sat on those low walls waiting for him to reach us. He took little evasive action, although on occasion he did walk up and down the middle of the street, stepping aside for the few cars and then shaking his fist and shouting after them. It all added to the sinister novelty of the man, and to the sense of our own bravery in confronting him like we did.

My mother suggested that he might have a family living nearby, a wife and children, perhaps, but I knew that this too was unlikely – his unkempt appearance, sloppy manners and dirty raincoat disproved that. He wore a shirt and tie beneath the coat, and these too were soiled and frayed, rubbing against his fat chin and fat hands. He sweated heavily, and constantly wiped his face and neck with a cloth the same colour as his coat. Often, beyond our reach, he would turn to face us and then deliver a longer, incomprehensible speech, telling us something none of us understood. Some of my friends said their parents said the man was a pervert and that he needed locking up for his own good.

Every time the man appeared, he was a challenge to our ignorance and our bravery. We threw small stones at him, always more to annoy than to actually injure him, and it sometimes occurred to me that the man seemed almost to accept this childish cruelty as the price of his presence among us.

We seldom followed him further than the fronts of our own homes, content once he had passed by to let him go on his way.

All of this came to a head one summer's day when the man, perhaps provoked beyond bearing, ran after a boy who tripped and fell on the road. The Pole pulled him to his feet and then held his face close and shouted at him, slapping him across his chest and shoulders. The boy screamed to be released and struggled against the man's grip. Eventually, the Pole let the boy go and he again fell to the ground. He crawled away a few yards before rising and running, pausing only when he was beyond the man's reach to shout back at him that he was going home to tell his father, who would in turn report him to the police. The Pole would learn his lesson and then finally get all that he had coming to him. Those of us watching understood how ineffectual any of these threats was likely to be.

The Pole clearly understood nothing of this and remained where he stood, regaining his composure and pulling his belt even tighter. He looked at the rest of us waiting nearby and shouted at us. We shouted back and then walked slowly away from him.

I told my mother what had happened and she said again that she felt sorry for the man. She told me she was disappointed in me and, as usual, I felt this keenly. My father repeated the common opinion that the man was everything people said he was, and that he did indeed deserve all he had coming to him.

The boy who had been grabbed reappeared among us the following day and showed off a small bruise on his arm. Someone said it was where he had fallen, but he insisted it was where the man had struck him. He said his father had every intention of going to the police when he could spare the time.

In the days that followed, the Pole himself reappeared on his walks. He seemed quieter, somehow subdued and he now crossed the road to avoid anyone on either pavement. The incident destroyed the mystery of the man, and though he continued to appear among us, we paid less and less attention to him, until at last, and without any of us noticing, he finally stopped passing back and forth among us.

44

I N the mid-seventies, due to events far beyond my under-standing and even further beyond my interest, the country was reduced to a three-day working week, and periodically the electricity to large areas of Sheffield was cut off. We had a gas fire and a gas cooker, but if the electricity which powered the local gas pumping station was cut off, then these appliances were also out of action.

Sheffield winters were never mild. Pipes and cisterns and toilets in every house I knew froze for days on end. No homes were insulated, few pipes were lagged. Windows were patterned with frozen condensation and ice crystals grew over their inside surfaces. Lead piping, which meant most piping, bulged, cracked and then eventually split and leaked at every thaw.

During the power cuts, shopkeepers rationed candles, and we were all dispatched to those shops further and further afield to try and build up a supply. A few drops of molten wax onto a saucer and the candle itself quickly and firmly pressed down on to this. The local newspapers printed timetables of where and when the power was going to be switched off over the coming week.

My Nan was by then living back on the Parson Cross estate, and because she was old – in her sixties – and would be living in the cold and the dark in her spotlessly clean home, I was sent to stay with her, travelling directly to and from school to her house on the estate, and sleeping on her settee because there was only a solitary narrow bed in the house.

The radio, television and lights clicked suddenly to life in the middle of the night, and my Nan came down at two in the morning to make a pot of tea for us both. Deprived earlier, she would be gasping. She drained the pot and then filled a flask and took this back upstairs with her. She had difficulty sleeping, she said, and her only real comfort was her supply of tea. That and her cigarettes. And who would begrudge her them?

When her cooker was out of action, we walked to the nearby chip shop and bought our meals there. She wouldn't allow these to be eaten in the street and so we carried them home to where our place-set stools were waiting.

She'd recently discovered a chip shop that sold curry sauce – had I ever tried it? No, of course I hadn't, what was she thinking? – and though it took some getting used to – just as all foreign food did – she savoured the exotic direction in which it pushed the chips and fish cakes made largely of potato and batter.

Staying with my Nan was an adventure for me, something considerably better than the claustrophobic, and now darkened, confines of my own home. I was away from my father, and for the first time in my life I was almost in control of things. Neither my Nan nor I could understand why, when row after row of houses were in complete darkness, the streetlights were still on. Something to do with road accidents, she imagined. She counted herself lucky to have a streetlight close to her own front door. Burglaries and assaults were reported to soar during the blackouts and we were all warned to be vigilant. I even imagined I was looking after her, though in truth I knew that the blackouts were nothing to her. At least there weren't German bloody bombers overhead putting honest, hardworking, decent people in fear of their mortal lives.

There were reports in the national newspapers pointing out that some people – *us*, in other words – were being forced to endure more than their fair share of the power cuts, while people living in other, better-off areas were suffering considerably less. Everybody knew somebody who had either fallen or walked into something in the dark. Everybody knew somebody else who had yet to suffer a single power cut.

My father predicted that because we lived so close to a large hospital, we would be spared. But we weren't. He swore blind that while we were sitting in complete darkness, people only a street away were well-lit and warm. Of all our deprivations in that house, the loss of the television was the greatest. He checked the paper to see which of his pubs were likely to be affected, and on what nights. It was a difficult routine to alter, but he did his best.

People complained that the city centre had night-long illuminated window displays. Council offices were invariably overlit and overheated, so where was the fairness in that? All right for some. How did a man in a factory somewhere, demanding to be paid more, result in my Nan living in darkness three or four afternoons or evenings every week? Water pressure was lost and so sinks and baths were filled in readiness. Common sense, really.

Sometimes the power went off when the cut wasn't scheduled and those hours of cold and dark seemed the unfairest of all.

My mother was again working full time by then, but neither she nor my father was cut back in their hours. After candles, batteries were rationed. The mahogany wireless with its usually glowing dial of a hundred cities no longer worked, but my small plastic and aluminium transistor radio still played pressed to my ear.

I went with my Nan on one of her regular visits to a nearby community centre and endured the simple and noisy jollity of all the other people her age enduring this latest calamity in their lives by drinking and singing and dancing and playing cards and bingo.

I was sitting my A levels at the time, and we were told at school that we should all make arrangements to ensure our revision timetables were not interrupted by the power cuts by arranging to go and stay with friends or relatives where the power remained on. I had never stayed with either friends or relatives overnight, except during rare family emergencies, and so the visits to my Nan's spotless home were something of an occasion.

Even when the power was off, my Nan told me this would make no difference to my exams, that I had the brains of the family in my head and that all I had to do now was to put them to good use. Brains alone, she said, would get me to wherever I wanted to be. I personally still had no idea of where or what that might be. No one in my family worked in any professional occupation, and the idea of attaining anything over that close horizon was still beyond my understanding. I was no good with my hands, slow on my feet, I didn't have a practical or a sporting bone in my body, but I was quick off the mark, I had those brains. Except this was never a clear or obvious advantage to me, not then – something, rather, always to be tempered with a measure of caution, denial and humility.

When that far-off strike and the power cuts finally ended, I reluctantly returned home to more revision and, finally, to my exams. I missed my Nan's settee and her small, pristine, polish-scented rooms. I missed the fish and chips and curry sauce and the sweet tea served in cups and saucers, the sugar in a bowl, the milk in a jug. I even missed the money she gave me, surreptitiously pressing the coins and folded notes into my hands and telling me to tell no one what she had given me, even though we were alone together in her house, sitting in the cold and the dark and counting down the minutes to the promised return of the warmth and the light.

45

O NCE a year, on a Saturday night at the height of summer, the Fine Fare had its annual staff outing, usually to a country pub and restaurant on the borders of the Peak District. Everyone attended, from the manager and his wife to the youngest shelf-stackers and Saturday boys. A coach picked us all up outside the supermarket an hour after closing and then delivered us back there in the early hours of the following morning.

The journey took an hour each way and the butchers and under-managers distributed bottles of drink the moment the coach started moving. It was a tradition of these outings that, after all the free drink had been consumed, none of the lowly paid shelf-stackers or Saturday boys would be allowed to buy their own drinks, but that these would be provided for them the whole of the evening by the rest of the staff.

I had never eaten in any kind of restaurant – nor knew anyone who had – before this; nor had I ever eaten a meal of four courses, let alone one served to me where I sat at a table surrounded by cutlery, crockery and glassware. Eating out was always considered an unnecessary extravagance, showing off, something normal people did not countenance. The only exception to this would be at the obligatory weddings, funerals and christenings we attended, where buffets – the word was always dramatically employed – of sandwiches, sausage rolls and pork pies were both expected and unvaried. The bulk of this laid-out food would anyway have been provided by the women attending these events. Shop-bought catering would have been frowned upon.

Like me, few of the shelf-stackers were true drinkers yet, and so in the face of unaccustomed generosity and variety, we all drank whatever we were offered. The butchers and under-managers made a great game of this, one in which we, their victims, were happily and encouragingly complicit.

After the meal, there was dancing, and the checkout girls and other women danced with us and clutched us to their perfumed busts. It was yet another part of the same game. Even the under-managers' wives and girlfriends danced with us, the teenagers, in front of their men.

The rooms in these country restaurants were large, decorated with the Fine Fare logo for the occasion, and had views out through the falling summer darkness of the Peak District hills or the Pennines beyond. Most places had a beer garden, another great novelty to us when compared to the yards and alleys of the city centre pubs.

To drink at the dinner table there were white and red wines in crystal glasses. People made short speeches and proposed toasts. It was easy to keep count of pints of drink, but not those served in different glasses and of varying strengths, especially when everything we were offered, we accepted. For once in our lives, we were being treated like grown-ups and so we tried to behave like them.

I attended three of these occasions, the last only a few weeks before I left home and Sheffield for good. I had never before been as drunk as I was on those summer Saturday nights, and seldom in the decades since.

The butchers made a joke of the whole event. Their short-skirted, cleavage-revealing wives and girlfriends flirted with us and then warned their men against giving us any more drink. Naturally, we objected to this and the women laughed and told us to suit ourselves. And just as I cannot remember being so drunk as on those nights, then seldom can I remember having been so happy. The men insisted there was no harm in us consuming so much drink, that we would have to find out about real drunkenness sooner or later, one way or another, so why not then? Besides, it was a private function, beyond the reach of the licensing laws. Plus, there was a coach and a driver waiting to deliver us all safely home.

As the evening progressed, the room darkened, the dancing continued and men went constantly back and forth to the bar. They were different to the company my father kept in his usual haunts – men who hardly spoke to each other except to comment on the drink, or weather, or work, or sport; men who ignored their wives and families completely once the pub door opened and the first drink was poured. These butchers, I decided again, were the men I most wanted to be like. Their women, too, were everything we boys might one day want for our own girlfriends and wives, but could then only fantasize about – glamorous, alluring, flirtatious, scented, *desirable*. These women put their arms around us and sat on our knees, whispered to us and kissed our cheeks as though it were the most natural thing in the world.

The evening ended at midnight when last orders were finally called. The coach was waiting in the car park. The toilets were filled and men lined the car park and pissed in lines into its grassy edges. Some were already the worse for wear, while others sought out the few remaining bottles for the journey back into the city.

And on that homeward journey, every one of the shelf-fillers and Saturday boys was sick, time after time after time. Sometimes the coach was able to stop and we wandered out into lay-bys and onto the moorland edges to be sick; at other times we retched into plastic Fine Fare shopping bags, which the manager always saw fit to bring. The coach filled with the sweet and acrid aroma of vomit, making us even sicker.

When the opportunity presented itself, the boys were gathered up by one of the older, more sensible women on board and taken outside. We were offered water, told to sit with our head between our knees. The sickness lasted the whole journey. The butchers and junior managers laughed at us and then complained at all the delays. Why, they asked us, did we insist on drinking so much if we couldn't hold it?

The journey finally at an end, we left the coach and settled ourselves on the raised flower beds in front of the supermarket. We were sick again. Arrangements were made for nearby parents to be called or boys delivered home. Lifts were offered by those still reasonably sober enough to drive. One by one we were all gathered up and returned home.

On the last occasion I attended, already turned eighteen, I insisted on being left where I sat with a friend as everyone else departed. It was by then almost two in the morning and I had no key to let myself back into the house.

My friend and I lied to the manager and told him someone was on their way to pick us up. The cold night air and two hours' respite from our near-continuous drinking was already starting to sober us up.

The pair of us fell asleep where we sat and were woken by the pealing of church bells at eight the following morning. We staggered to my friend's nearby home and pretended to his own church-going parents that we'd spent the night on their settee and armchair so as not to wake anyone.

I then waited until I knew my father would be out on his own Sunday lunchtime drinking session before walking the mile or so home. I told my mother that I'd stayed with my friend and that his parents had been happy to accommodate me. She hoped I hadn't been any trouble, that I hadn't shown myself – meaning her – up.

Later, I described to her everything I'd eaten at the four-course meal. I told her about the various pieces of cutlery, the different glasses for different drinks, the jugs of water at each table, the napkins we'd laid in our laps. She made sure I'd remembered to thank everybody for including me in the occasion. I reassured her that I had, and that, no, I hadn't made a fool of myself by drinking too much. Because we all knew where that led.

When she next put my best shirt in the wash she sniffed at it and I lied again and told her that the boy sitting next to me on the coach had been sick. She found a wine cork in one of my pockets and I patiently explained to her that when people ate out at proper restaurants they often kept these as souvenirs.

46

THROUGHOUT my childhood and adolescence I had a moderate talent and a great fondness for drawing, more often than not panoramic battle scenes containing hundreds of tiny figures and dozens of explosions. My growing collection of Airfix models made my depiction of aircraft, tanks, warships and all manner of weaponry and uniforms more than competent. I enjoyed my time alone with pencils and paper. It was only when I bought myself an oil painting kit that I discovered the true limits of both my talent and my capabilities. In truth, I got more satisfaction from completing a painting-by-numbers kit, one of which usually turned up with my name on it at Christmas or my birthday. The completed paintings were dutifully displayed somewhere on our walls, often fighting the elaborate wallpaper behind. Eventually, these artworks were taken down and stacked either on top of or in the bottom of my bedroom wardrobe, where the detritus of all our lives seemed to settle.

At school I did well in my art classes, my colour blindness becoming more of an asset than a hindrance. Trees *were* red in some light, leaves *were* blue. I began to consider myself an artist, someone with an artistic vision, my prowess endlessly on display to be admired by everyone fortunate enough to see it.

In contrast to my lack of musical, even singing ability, my art provided me with a focus. It was a solitary endeavour, and though being alone in that house – let alone being alone and quiet and undisturbed – was a rare event, I snatched every moment I could, eventually moving from my shared bedroom down into the cellar to draw and paint.

My favourite drawings were scenes I remembered from films I'd seen. I went to see *Zulu*, *Waterloo*, *Custer's Last Stand*, *The Charge of the Light Brigade*, *Lawrence of Arabia* and countless other productions featuring vast set-piece battles, and afterwards I spent days constructing meticulous A5 miniatures of similar scenes. Horses charged and fell, mutilated by cannon shot, cavalrymen skirmished amid gathering Redskins, Mitsubishi Zeroes strafed among racing landing craft, the Light Brigade was blown to smithereens. All in minute, gory detail.

My pleasure in all of these violent horrors knew no bounds. When, at the age of sixteen or seventeen, my model-making mania finally ran out of steam, I took dozens of my badly glued and painted aeroplanes and tanks and soldiers and destroyed them with fire and fireworks. I emptied gunpowder from split-open bangers into fuselages and hulls and turrets and concocted fuses made of parcel string soaked in lighter fuel. I packed soldiers into bunkers and half-tracks where they burned and melted to death. I did most of this in the back garden when no one was watching. The black and pungent smoke of burning plastic quickly filled the cellar before finding its way out via the coal grate.

Music arrived in my life and I started buying records, 45s mostly, but with precious albums slowly accumulating, mostly second-hand, swapped and traded with other boys. My record collection became my prize possession, small though it remained, and kept well away from my parents' own random and haphazardly accumulated collection – the *West Side Story* soundtrack, Andy Williams, Lulu, Tony Bennett, the Everly Brothers, Cilla Black, Benny Hill, the Beatles. I knew all the words to 'Moon River', but not what a Moon River might actually be – a river on the moon, presumably, and I knew *that* was unlikely – and only able to guess at what might constitute a Huckleberry Friend. *We're off to see the world, there's such a lot of world to see. Here he comes, that's Cathy's Clown. I want to be* – dum dum – *Bobby's Girl. Anyone who had a heart...*

My father arrived home one evening with an eight-track cartridge player and so we listened over and over to the Carpenters, Gilbert O'Sullivan, Tony Christie, Tom Jones, Shirley Bassey, Engelbert Humperdink – those same singers who might even have performed at the club only six doors away.

I took down my Aircraft of the World posters and put up posters of David Bowie and others. My father told me that if I wasn't careful I'd find myself turning into a man just like him, and whatever else I might think I wanted in Life, I didn't want *that*. I found a sheep's skull and painted it with a red and silver blaze, just like Bowie had on the *Aladdin Sane* album. *Now* what was I up to? For somebody who was supposed to be clever, I didn't show much sign of it. I put up a poster in which Bowie's tightly clad genitals featured prominently. I needed watching, I really did. Just imagine the shame if I *did* turn out to be one of *them*. I even found myself wishing I *was* one of them just to punish my father. The indignity and loss of face would be unbearable to him. He'd read all those stories in his *News of the World*, he knew all the signs, knew what to look out for, so not much got past him. And besides which, no son of *his* was setting off down that particular path, not if he had anything to do with it, which he did, and whether *I* liked it or not. And if I didn't like it, then I could lump it and get used to it. I might have been fifteen or sixteen or seventeen, but he still knew best, and certainly what was best for me, what was best for us all. And if there was anything I still didn't like about his way of doing things, then I always knew where the door was. There was always that.

47

A GIRL I'd known at Hucklow Road School went missing. Her face appeared on the front page of the *Sheffield Star* for several consecutive nights. Her parents appeared on the local evening news bulletins, sitting close together on their settee, her mother crying, her father with his stiff arm around the woman; the girl's younger brothers and sisters stood beside the couple, some as tearful as their mother; others looked simultaneously terrified and excited by all the attention they were so suddenly receiving.

The girl's name was Shirley. The photograph in the evening paper showed her when she was eleven or twelve; she was now fifteen. It was a school photograph, in which she was scrubbed and smiling, her hair fastened back in a plait, her home-knit cardigan buttoned to her neck. All of which made her appear considerably younger than she'd looked when I'd last seen her a week or two earlier.

Appeals were made, searches undertaken. The family lived on the main road leading from Page Hall to Firth Park. There was a large park across the road, and a narrow strip of wooded slope on the same side as Shirley's home. A few hundred yards further back lay the uninhabited ridge of Wincobank, with its as-yet undemolished estate of derelict wartime prefabs. Few of the actual buildings stood intact, but the scrubby, crater- and scrap-filled site was scattered with their concrete foundations. They were all scrupulously searched and everyone was questioned. A few people were reported to have been taken to the local police stations and interviewed there. No one had anything to reveal.

Shirley's disappearance remained a perplexing and unsettling mystery to us all. People visited her parents. They said Shirley's mother was neither eating nor sleeping. All she did now, apparently, was cry. Shirley's father insisted that his daughter was alive and well somewhere, and he appealed to her to get in touch with the family, if only for her mother's sake. He told her and the watching viewers that she wasn't in any trouble and that all she had to do now was to let them know where she was; no one was angry at her, no one was going to punish her for everything she was putting them through. Anything to put her poor mother's mind at rest.

The paper said Shirley was taller than most girls her age and that she also looked older. A new photograph was printed – one in which she did indeed look much older than that awkwardly smiling schoolgirl.

Then it was pointed out to the police by one of her friends that, despite her age, Shirley already had a boyfriend, and that he was at least three years older than Shirley. The youth was found and interviewed, but he too professed to having no idea where Shirley had gone, why she had run off like that.

In the more recent photograph, Shirley was wearing make-up – lipstick and eye-liner. Shirley's father told a local reporter that he hardly recognized his own daughter. The family did not own a telephone, but the public were urged to call any police station in the city with information concerning the runaway girl. The word added both glamour and daring to her disappearance.

Fearful speculation was rife. My mother asked me when I'd last seen Shirley, if she'd said anything to me. But I knew nothing, except that the girl had long since outgrown most of us who had known her at Hucklow Road School. None of us even knew or suspected that she had a boyfriend, let alone that he was so much older than her. The rest of us were still children compared to that. Growing children, already drinking and smoking, perhaps, but still children testing that same uncertain and eagerly anticipated territory ahead of us.

All the usual speculations were made and repeated and embellished upon. My father said it sold newspapers. His own were full of girls who'd disappeared from home. And we all knew what *that* was all about. There was even a feature on Shirley herself in the same paper, weeks after her disappearance. And those of us who *didn't* know what that was all about were either too blind or too stupid or just burying our heads in the sand. My mother told him not to talk like that in front of his children, anxious that we might repeat what he'd said.

We waited for Shirley's body to be found, most likely in the woods or the park, even more likely on the messy slopes of Wincobank. We waited for a man to be arrested who would then confess to the terrible things he'd done to her. You didn't even have to guess or speculate about those things – it was there every Sunday in black and white, obvious to anybody with a pair of eyes and a brain in their head. Sex, probably; nudity certainly; possibly even torture or at least tying-up. Something that had started out in all innocence, perhaps, and then gone too far, gone badly wrong, as these things often did. There would be a photograph of the body, or at least a shot of the overgrown, concrete-strewn ground where it had finally been found; followed eventually by a mug shot of the man who had been arrested, tried and convicted of her murder. Make no mistake, these men were always out there, forever prowling among the innocent and the curious and waiting for their chance.

And time passed. No body was found. There were occasional further articles in the newspapers, local and national, saying that the missing girl had been spotted. Spotted in London – always London – and then afterwards, perhaps, definitely, almost definitely, in Manchester, Leeds, Barnsley, Doncaster, Rotherham. The list of these sightings grew as both hope and expectation slowly faded.

And then, months after Shirley's disappearance, there was another report in the local paper suggesting that Shirley, at the time of her disappearance, might – *might*, mind you, just might – have been pregnant with her older boyfriend's baby. And if that was the case, then that altered everything. Of course it did. London was mentioned again. It remained a foreign country to us. A country where runaways ran to, and where all sorts of things might then happen to those runaways. Runaways, beaten children, accused thieves, bullied runts, pregnant schoolgirls. It was even suggested that Shirley's parents had known of their daughter's pregnancy all along and that they had conspired to keep this from both the police and the public. What else would you do? Bad enough that your daughter had run away from home, and all the shame and suspicion that *that* had brought down on her poor parents' heads. But *pregnant*? Sex. An underage girl. Sex with an older boy. A man. A man who had taken liberties, taken advantage. A man who should have known better. Her boyfriend swore blind that all this was untrue, and if it was true, then that he definitely wasn't the father.

No wonder she'd run away. Her poor mother. How was *she* ever going to live with all that? Next thing we'd hear, my father predicted, would be the stupid, thoughtless, feckless girl selling her side of the story to the newspapers and causing her parents even more distress. Followed, no doubt, by weeping and wailing all round – Come Home Shirley, all was forgiven, a new grandmother desperate to see her first grandchild. She puts everyone through hell, he said – not to mention the cost to the police – and then that same stupid, thoughtless, feckless girl was allowed to return home – and who pays for that particular ticket? – and then be welcomed back into the loving embrace of her family. *Loving embrace*? Don't make him laugh. The girl might have ruined her own life, and that of her child's, but who was counting? She was home now, and that was all that mattered. The newspapers must be rubbing their hands: two stories for the price of one, more.

The truth of the matter was revealed to us over the years ahead in small, insignificant-seeming details, facts grown old and blunt and no longer able to shock.

Shirley had indeed become pregnant, and she had run away to London to hide this. The boyfriend again swore on oath that he had never slept with her and so the baby was not his. One mystery was dismissed out of hand; another slowly evaporated and was forgotten.

And that was the last any of us heard of Shirley. We looked at her house when we passed it on the bus or when we played in the park opposite. We pointed out her mother and father and brothers and sisters when they walked alongside us in the street, but other than that we avoided them. Even my mother agreed that there was considerably more to that particular little story than people were letting on.

The greatest mystery to me was how a fourteen-year-old girl – whatever her predicament, however desperate – could simply get on either a coach or a train bound for distant London, get off there and then, to all intents and purposes, completely disappear from view and move so swiftly beyond all contact. The world I knew and lived in was such a solid, familiar, predictable place, its boundaries inviolate.

And so perhaps Shirley and her baby would make new lives for themselves. Perhaps all would be forgiven, everything resolved, and everybody would one day be happy. Perhaps the unknown father would stand by his family; perhaps he wouldn't. Perhaps Social Services had already taken the baby into care. Perhaps Shirley would see her child again; perhaps she wouldn't. Perhaps her parents would discover where she was living, seek her out and bring her home with them. Perhaps Shirley would miraculously turn back into the girl she had once been and then resume her education. Perhaps her parents would bring the baby up as their own; stranger things had happened.

That world and all its certainties might tip on its axis occasionally, but it always somehow righted itself. Wrong-doing was always sought out, always discovered, judged and punished; we all knew that.

I certainly never saw Shirley again. Nobody I knew ever saw her again. Not only wasn't there a happy ending to the story of the runaway, underage, pregnant schoolgirl, but it seemed to me that there wasn't any kind of ending whatsoever.

48

WHILE our annual seaside holiday was the highlight of our year as a family, for me the journey there and back formed no part of that pleasure. I was badly travel sick as a child, and whatever old wives' remedy might have been attempted each year, none was successful. Even if pharmaceutical remedies had been available, I was given none. The cars my father drove were filled with the smells of petrol, oil, leather upholstery and cigarette smoke. I was forced to sit in the rear with my brother and sister, often with luggage on our knees and with boxes of food at our feet.

The trick, I was told, was not to look out of the side window at the landscape flashing by, but to position myself at the centre of the back seat and look directly ahead, out of the windscreen. The disadvantage of this was that when I did start to feel sick – frequently only ten miles into our ninety-mile journey – I then felt trapped, unable even to reach a window or door and climb quickly out.

The nausea was overpowering, and once the first of its symptoms was felt there could only ever be one outcome. I pleaded to sit in the front, but, in such an overcrowded space, this was impossible. My father was the only driver, my mother sat beside him and we children in the rear. This natural order was never changed. There were no seatbelts in the front or rear to further restrict anyone, but getting out was always a lengthy, awkward procedure.

I was given plastic bags to be sick into, but the simple fact of knowing this uncertain solution to the problem was at hand only made matters worse for me, seeming to bring forward the first of those symptoms.

Once we had departed, our route carefully planned, my father was unhappy at having to make any unscheduled diversion or halt. Even a few minutes' delay would throw his timings out. The only reason he finally did this was because it was preferable to me throwing up over myself and our luggage and, worst of all, over the inside of his recently cleaned car.

I would tell him when I felt the first of the symptoms and he would judge where the best place to stop on the road ahead of us might be. I would not be allowed to embarrass us all by getting out and throwing up anywhere we might be publicly observed. On most of the road, he said, it was either impossible or too dangerous to stop. What we really needed was an overgrown lay-by. Preferably an empty one, and preferably one screened from the road.

Eventually, and often with my hands over my mouth and liquid already seeping, I was pushed and pulled out of the car and pointed toward a bush or a clump of nettles and dock. I was told to get a move on and to be sure to get everything out. He wasn't going to be stopping again and delaying us even further. I was told to lean forward to ensure nothing went on my holiday clothes; nobody wanted to sit with the smell of sick in that warm car. We carried a roll of toilet paper for me to wipe my mouth and hands. Once outside, I was told to breathe deeply – country air being a cure for most things – in the certain knowledge that this would either settle my nausea or encourage the vomit.

I was told to walk up and down, preferably away from the car. If nothing came up immediately, I was told to stick a finger down my throat. And all the time I was following these instructions I was conscious of the other motorists and their families who might also have stopped in the lay-by on the way to their own holidays, some of whom might even have been brewing up a pot of tea on a primus stove. How many other holidays did I want to ruin?

I was acutely aware that every minute I stood there, desperate to get everything over and done with, I was making us late. Every minute I was being sick, causing a delay, confounding my father's timetable, then the road to the sea was filling up; or perhaps an accident was taking place somewhere along those miles ahead and we were going to be delayed even further.

Unsurprisingly, the fresh air *did* make me feel briefly better, but this was hardly an advantage, and certainly not the cure or blessing it might have been. I cooled down after the heat of the car. The sweat of my palms and on the back of my legs evaporated. I breathed deeply, testing my responses. Perhaps this *was* finally going to be the year when I wasn't sick at all, when I didn't spoil it for everyone else. My overriding understanding during all this time spent waiting for the inevitable was that I was at least outside the car, my father's pride and joy, and that whatever happened now, it would not make my father any angrier than he already was. It was, after all, our holiday week – the one week in the year when *nothing* was supposed to frustrate him or make him angry.

When the vomit did finally come, it was wet and thin and tasted bitter. This was followed by a few minutes' dry retching, during which there was little more to bring up. After this, I would wipe myself on the toilet paper, check my hands and chin and clothing and then stand for a moment breathing deeply in that restorative air.

We wouldn't be stopping a second time, I was informed. I usually felt exhausted after the vomiting, my head light, my balance off. I felt as though I had survived an ordeal. The taste of the bile was in my mouth for long afterwards. There was nothing for me to rinse with; besides, whatever I might drink would only bring back the nausea. There would be giant bottles of pop in our food supplies, but these were for the holiday, and that only started once we had arrived at the holiday camp and had been allocated our caravan or chalet.

I remembered places where I had been sick in previous years and felt triumphant when we passed them, only to have to pull up a few miles further on for the whole painful process to begin anew.

One year – I was about fifteen – I travelled further than ever, perhaps even over the halfway mark, and as I left the car and wandered along the overgrown verge of a stone wall, I genuinely believed that this year *was* going to be different, that I *wasn't* going to be sick, that I *was* going to walk away from the car, breathe deeply for a minute or two, perhaps even make a few exploratory jabs with my finger, and that I would then return to my waiting family in triumph.

I had finally grown out of being car sick, just like everyone had told me I would. It was a thing of childhood, something which existed only to be left behind, proof, perhaps, that my childhood was ending. But then there was the unavoidable thought that perhaps, having grown a year older, all I had done was survive the first surge of nausea. I would then get back in the car, only to have the same thing happen again ten minutes later. Not only would I *not* have started my eventual recovery, but I would actually have made things far worse. It also occurred to me that if my father was angry upon our arrival at the holiday camp, then his anger might somehow cling to him beyond that sacred boundary.

On that occasion, to make entirely certain that I finally wasn't going to be sick, I walked a few yards further and climbed a low bank to look over the stone wall there, breathing deeply and gazing out across the countryside beyond. And as I did this something sickly and sharp caught my nose and I looked down to see, a few feet below me, the rotting carcase of a dead sheep, its head intact, its bloated body covered with grey, matted wool, and its open stomach heaving with a mass of writhing maggots. Within seconds I was retching and then throwing up, unexpectedly pleased that this was finally happening and that I might now return to the car confident that the rest of our journey would not be interrupted.

49

FOLLOWING my grandfather's death, my Nan remarried. In the meantime, she'd left her Parson Cross council house, been rehoused on the seventh floor of a block of flats on the far side of the city, and then later been brought back to the estate into a home almost identical to her first.

It was here that she met Joe. They socialized together in local pubs and clubs, then they began courting, and then they got married in a Registry Office, both of them almost seventy, both of them pensioners.

Companionship, someone to talk to, someone to cook for, someone to worry over, someone to clean for, someone to cajole and keep on the straight and narrow, someone to care for and to love. From Jack to Joe. It was a straightforward, reassuring and happy arrangement. I knew of no one else in our entire family who had remarried. Joe gave up his own council house and moved in with her. Like Jack before him, he did the garden and all the outdoor work, while she continued to dust, wipe, polish, scrub, wash and vacuum everything indoors to its usual gleaming and perfectly ordered spotlessness.

Joe had a glass eye, which he told us was the result of an explosion. A tap of his nose, Army compo. He took the eye out and showed it to us, but none of us dared hold it. Every time we saw him he told us he would keep his eye out for us and laughed louder than anyone else. He said he removed the eye each night and dropped it into one of his socks for safe-keeping and so that he'd know precisely where it was in the dark of the following morning as he dressed for work. He said my Nan polished it once a week and that his eyesight had never been so good. Like all of my relatives, he told these same few stories of himself over and over. They were stories we enjoyed hearing and they connected us to the man. Tell them about how you lost your eye, Joe. God knows how many of his oppos might have caught a packet if he and his two good eyes hadn't thrown themselves in harm's way.

One day, he told us, the bastards who were sergeants woke them all up in the middle of the night and set them off on a twenty-mile run. Thing is, he hadn't had time to fish his glass eye out of his sock and pop it back into its socket. The result of this was that he ran and marched twenty miles with the eye in his boot, resulting in the biggest blister the Army had ever seen, every step an agony. It was the tale we most enjoyed hearing and we never risked spoiling that pleasure by considering its inconsistencies and improbabilities.

Joe laughed at himself when he told us the tales and he seemed overall a much more cheerful man than her first husband, who my father nicknamed Jolly Jack on account of his dour and taciturn nature.

Occasionally, Joe and my Nan came on holiday with us. Joe, after a lifetime of early shifts, always woke early, got up, clattered around the chalet brewing tea, smoking and making himself bacon sandwiches. He then sat on the small porch doing a tabloid crossword, having been the camp shop's first customer as the doors were opened and the papers taken in at dawn. The crossword took him minutes and gave him great satisfaction. He wasn't an educated man, he told us, but he had quick wits. Being the confirmed brainbox of the family, I was often asked how to spell certain words.

There were few answers of more than five or six letters, and when Joe proudly showed me the completed puzzle, I saw that he had filled in the squares with any words that fitted and interlocked, frequently altering the spelling of those that did not properly mesh. When I told him that this was not how crosswords were supposed to be done, he tapped his nose and said, So what? It was how *he* did them, and where was the harm in that? As long as you got the thing done, that was all that counted. Nobody ever got anywhere without bending and breaking a few rules every now and again. If life had taught him anything, it had taught him that. Another finger tapped against his nose.

When Joe died, leaving my Nan alone again, I'd already been gone from home for four or five years. Someone called to tell me that he'd died and that the funeral had already taken place, that there had been no need for me to attend. After all, they said, he hadn't been my *real* grandfather.

50

I N my mid-teens, I grew as tall as my father and then an inch taller. Until that point, he'd regularly insisted on the pair of us standing back to back in our stockinged feet while my mother compared our heights. That extra inch surprised him. But whatever I might *think* it signified, he quickly told me, I'd do well to remember that I'd never be half the man he was. Not now, not ever. I might be five feet nine and a half inches to his five feet eight and a half inches, but that extra inch counted for nothing when compared to everything *he*'d been through in life, everything *he*'d done, seen and endured. I might finally have got that extra inch, he said, but what was it compared to all that?

My mother was careful in her own assessment of that inch. It stood to reason, she said, that I would one day be taller than he was – because he'd provided everything I needed to grow that barely noticeable bit taller, whereas he had never… I stopped listening to her. As far as I was concerned, he was still living that separate, angry life in parallel to the rest of us and she was still making those same excuses for him, forever interpreting that restless anger and capricious violence into a language none of us ever truly understood.

Around that time, I bought a pair of headphones and sat

in my bedroom listening to the same few records over and over, anything to remove myself even further from him and to begin to form my own, separate identity in that claustrophobic space.

By sixteen or seventeen, I was at last starting to identify a vague course ahead of me. If *he* could lead that separate existence in our midst, then why not me?

We were all growing, of course, but as far as I was concerned, my sister and brother remained children, and still under his control.

He had told us often enough how unfair life had been to him, how all the hardship and misfortune he had endured had made him into the man he had become. But now, or so it seemed to me, in my mid-teen years, he, despite his angry denials and constant boasting, had done absolutely nothing whatsoever to alter the forming of that thirty-eight-year-old man. He was still angry, still venting that anger on everyone but himself, still uncomfortable in his own skin.

He had once been a funny man, forever telling jokes and making amusing remarks about the people and events around him. These were all too often cruel and scathing remarks, but still funny. And, we all knew, if he was being funny and people were laughing at what he said, then at least he wasn't being angry. If people were encouraging him and laughing with him, then he was unlikely to be cruel or judgemental toward *them*. We all had our failings in that family, and he always had these to hand. Anything that kept him from exposing those failings, especially in company, was a bonus.

At seventeen, I occasionally accompanied my father to his pubs and bars. At the time, this seemed almost a reward to me, and certainly something to be savoured and enjoyed.

He congratulated me on the occasion when I was picked up along with half a dozen of my adolescent friends for under-age drinking. A plainclothes policeman came to the house to deliver an unofficial warning to me. My mother was mortified at the appearance of the man and she agreed to everything he suggested regarding my future behaviour. He left her a leaflet to study. My father, on the other hand, nodded along with the man while he was there and then swore at him as his footsteps receded along the passageway. I was a chip off the old block, he told me. He punched me on the shoulder and I did all I could to prevent myself flinching at his touch.

My mother, while she continued to both reassure and com-fort her children following my father's more violent outbursts, still refused to openly confront the man. Their mutual reliance on each other remained strong, but gradually, as we all grew older, my father's dependence on his wife increased, tipping the balance in her favour: he still could not cook himself a meal or shop for food; he had never washed or ironed a piece of clothing in his life; he had never swept or polished or dusted a room or piece of furniture; he had never once stripped and then re-made a bed.

In many ways, the material concerns of our family life improved: the televisions got larger, the furniture became more modern, more stylish; we ate meals from packets prepared by someone else; the new gas cooker included an ignition button, the paraffin heaters disappeared.

Sadly, little of this seemed to offer any degree of true con-tentment or sense of achievement to my father: he still boasted of everything he acquired for us, still insisted on our approval and admiration. But everything about him was beginning to wear thin. He started to gain weight. He remained a vain, self-regarding man, but slowly he became less showy; he still wore his jewellery, but nothing as eye-catching as his earlier pieces. He abandoned the gold sleeve restraints and started wearing two-tone cardigans with leather buttons and suede front panels.

He frequently told all his children he'd be glad to see the back of them, because then, he said, he and my mother would finally be able to start treating themselves to the better things in life, to the things they *deserved*. I didn't understand what these things might be. A caravan of their own, he said. And that was just for starters. Trips out into the countryside without kids throwing up left, right and centre. Benidorm for weeks on end in winter when they were finally pensioners twenty-five years in the future. My sister would be leaving school soon enough – let's face it, *she* certainly wouldn't be wasting her time by staying on until she was eighteen – followed three years later by my brother. Big changes, and all to the good.

Once – and only once – in an uncharacteristically frank, albeit maudlin, admission to me, sitting together in the car outside our home after a night's drinking, he admitted to me that he should never have had children – something else his own mother had once told him, told everyone, all those years ago. It had all been a mistake, he said, and now it was too late to do anything about it. The life he had once wanted for himself had disappeared behind him without him noticing. First the death of his parents, then the Army, then his marriage and then the children. One thing had simply led to another and there was nothing anyone could have done about that; it was how life worked. My mother might have been a good – a *natural* – mother, he admitted, but the same could never in a million years be said of his own attempts at fatherhood. I had little notion then that he might actually have been jealous of his own children, angry that the love, affection, concern and attention that he considered to be rightly his, and his alone, had for so long been diverted away from him.

I, too, was half-drunk at the time of this rare confession – my limits in the pub more quickly reached than his – and I told him that it didn't matter. I was embarrassed and caught off-guard by what he'd said. I told him he'd done his best. I didn't believe it for a moment, but it was what I said. It was an awkward moment of near-intimacy between us, and all I wanted then was for it to pass, to get out of the smoke-filled car and to suck in the sobering cold night air. But he himself seemed reluctant to go back into the house, and for a painful moment, I thought that for the first time in his life he was going to attempt to embrace me.

51

W HEN I was seventeen I sat my A levels. English, English Literature, Geography and Art. I passed Geography and Art, two B grades, and failed both the English exams. The following year, I re-sat English alongside General Studies and acquired a further two B's. Four B's. I was going to university in Hull.

I had filled in all the forms a year earlier and been given a conditional offer of those four B's.

I had no true idea of what going to university entailed, what I was intended to do there, how I was meant to live, how hard I would be expected to work, what I was intended to achieve or what this might mean with regard to my life ahead.

No one else in my extended family or in the families of my friends or neighbours had ever been educated beyond the age of eighteen; most had left school at the first opportunity two and more years before that. Certainly, no one I knew had ever gone to university. There had been a few technical college courses, night schools, perhaps, but I knew little of them.

In those days, most people I knew left school on Friday afternoon and started their working lives as apprentices or labourers or office clerks the following Monday morning. A cliché but also a truth. One of the first things I had been told – promised, almost – upon being notified that I had passed my eleven-plus and would be going to grammar school was that I could now look forward to a cushy little number at a desk in an office somewhere rather than down on one of those hot and dirty factory floors where all those other less-well-educated men and women would be spending their own working lives.

I chose to study Geography at university – not because of any genuine devotion, fondness or aptitude for the subject – a subject that anyway proved to be considerably different to the one I had studied at school – but because it seemed the most practical line to follow. Where did studying English Literature ever get anyone? What even *was* General Studies? And Art? *Art?*

A year earlier, following a school visit, I had been offered a place at an art college close to Sheffield city centre. I had taken along a portfolio of my work and had been offered the place a week later. I turned it down. Going to the college would have been little different from going to school. I would have taken a bus there and back each day and continued to live at home and share a bunk bed with my twelve-year-old brother. To me, the whole point of going to university was to get away from home. Whatever else university might prove to be, and whatever it might demand of me, it would at least in no way resemble the home and the life I would be leaving behind.

I applied to go to Hull for the same reason I made my four other choices – because none of the places demanded a Maths O level, which I had failed two years previously, along with Biology, Physics and Chemistry. I was no scientist. I re-sat the Maths and failed it a second and then a third time. I was even less of a mathematician.

I visited Hull, two hours away by two trains, and made my decision. I was offered a room in a hall of residence and I accepted this, too. I made all these connections and commitments to what lay ahead of me still without any true understanding of what any of them meant. I applied for, and was awarded, a grant by Sheffield Education Authority to cover my living expenses and to allow me ten pounds a week on top of that. It was a fortune to me. Who couldn't live on ten pounds a week?

52

A ROUND the same time, my father became more relaxed about wearing his wig. He would still ritually remove it upon his return each evening and then sit around bald-headed on the nights he remained at home, but now he seldom jumped from his chair and rushed upstairs each time the alarm of footsteps sounded in the passageway leading to our back door.

Additionally, he started to experiment with letting his own sparse wreath of hair grow longer. Wearing the wig meant that he was forced to regularly trim this, his own hair, so that no unnatural-looking bumps appeared beneath the thin weave of the hairpiece. Crown Topper even sold him the long, slender scissors to achieve this, as though, yet again, only their own expensive brand would do the job properly.

He even began to suggest that perhaps, having worn the wig for so long, it was now actually *preventing* his own natural growth from recurring. And, in truth, there did appear to be more of his own hair sprouting across his pale scalp. Still thin and sparse, perhaps, still restricted to the wreath around his ears and the back of his skull, but almost certainly more; enough, even, for the occasional comb-over or experimentation with forward combing; but, sadly for him, never quite enough to replicate what his wig achieved; never enough to allow him to finally dispense with the thing. The Crown Topper people, I imagined, would have included this eventual regrowth in the list of their product's benefits, perhaps even declaring it some kind of miracle.

Now when people came to the house, he sat without moving as they entered. And just as very few had commented on his wig-wearing to begin with, so few remarked now on the reappearance of his own balding head. Besides, he said, still trying to convince himself more than anyone listening, he was growing older, approaching his forties, and many men of that age were starting to lose their hair.

Both his brothers had identical hairstyles and then hair loss, and to see the three men together had only ever made the dramatic change in his own appearance more remarkable and obvious. Perhaps, he told us, the time had come to dispense with the toupee once and for all. My mother, her usual cautious, conciliatory self, told him it made no difference whatsoever to her, and we children knew well enough by then how to read the signals and to agree with everything he said. As usual, the line of least resistance was always the preferred option in that household.

He started to complain about the cost of maintaining the wig, convincing himself further that its time was nearing an end. New weaves had appeared during those six years; slight changes of colour, of hair thickness; even the polystyrene head had been replaced a few times. Besides, he added, as his own hair greyed prematurely, the so-called experts at Crown Topper were adding the same washed-out colours to his hairpiece. Even *he* could see the logic in abandoning an expensive wig deliberately designed to make him look old before his time.

He frequently reminded us of the age at which his own father had died – thirty-eight – and of the years and months he had now outlived the man. Perhaps enough was enough. Besides, who in their right mind actually wanted a full head of grey hair? More to the point, who wanted a head of expensively created and still-obviously-a-wig grey hair?

And so, just as the wig had come into our lives and governed our routines and created its alarms and urgencies in that house, it now went. We drove off on holiday one year, back to our beloved Flamborough Head chalet, and the wig stayed on its smooth white head on the dressing table in the bedroom. Even the holidaymakers who remembered us from previous years did not remark on the difference.

The comb-overs and forward-combs represented a period of transition for my father. He went to work without his wig, came home, and then went back the next day. Mostly, the people who hadn't laughed at him then didn't laugh at him now. Presumably, the people who *had* smirked behind their hands all those years ago did the same now, but again he contrived not to notice them.

He was asked occasionally why he no longer wore his wig and he affected a casual lack of concern, disdain even, for the thing. He told people it was just something he'd tried out, but that now he was trying out something different. He tried to make himself sound like a man who might do that kind of thing.

The wig went from the polystyrene head into a dressing-table drawer. I asked him for the head and then painted it. Later, as it crumbled into small balls with too much handling, I threw it away.

And so the wig left our lives. We no longer had to lie and pretend; our relatives no longer had to lie and pretend; and likewise all his workmates and drinking companions, friend and foe alike.

It was a weight off his shoulders, he said. It was a joke. My mother prompted us to make encouraging remarks, just as we had all been prompted to do when the wig had first arrived. I made my share of comments, but by then I was past caring about the man or his feelings. Our lives as father and son had long since diverged, and I was determined that they would diverge even further and faster once I left home in a few months' time.

We went to the usual family gatherings, where jokes were occasionally made about the vanished wig. A few awkward or unguarded remarks might have been made by drinking men, but these usually passed without any serious or lasting conflicts arising. Besides, there were always those sensible, sober women present – sisters and sisters-in-law mostly – who forever acted as comforters and peacemakers amid the tribe of their husbands.

By the time I left home at eighteen, the wig no longer featured in our lives. They were not happier, more relaxed lives as a consequence of this, just wigless lives. I grew my own hair into a variety of fashionable and ridiculous styles; suedehead, mullet and soft quiff came and went. And short-back-and-sides remained the cheapest remedy for all these experimental failures, always another starting point from which anything was possible according to a teenager's endlessly shifting obsessions.

Some of my friends shaved their heads; others grew their hair long over their shoulders. We joined our own emerging tribes. Some even attempted sparse moustaches. Anything on my own upper lip always looked like dust or dried food. And the last thing I wanted was for people to look at me the way they had looked at my father's wig.

53

O n the day of my departure for Hull, a Saturday in late September, 1974, my father, in an uncharacteristic act of generosity, offered to drive me there. I packed my small canvas school bag with most of what little I owned and said my brief and unmemorable goodbyes. What would be the point of anything more effusive when I'd be back to visit in less than a month? My mother stayed at home to look after my brother and sister.

The journey was a long one, mostly silent. Neither my father nor I could really discuss or even speculate on what lay ahead of me. And so, as usual, we talked about other drivers, the state of the traffic, the state of the roads, the largely unknown route ahead of us both.

We arrived in Hull, located the University, and then my father drove us to the nearest pub. I went in with him and we drank two or three pints together. Leaving, he took money from his wallet and gave it to me. I pretended to refuse it, but he insisted, pushing it into my pocket. It would come in useful, he said. Besides, who didn't need a few extra nicker every now and then? Put it away; I was embarrassing him. If he'd learned one lesson in life, it was that everything, absolutely everything, one way or another, cost more than you thought.

Afterwards, he drove me to the University entrance, added a bottle of whisky and a carton of two hundred cigarettes – don't tell your mother; plenty more where that came from – to the little I had already packed, shook my hand, wished me well, said he'd better set off to avoid the traffic and drove alone back to Sheffield.

I found the room I had been allocated and let myself in. The room was spartan, undecorated, unembellished. It looked as though no one had ever lived there before me, as though I were its first occupant. It contained a fitted wardrobe with space for ten times what I had brought with me, a bed, a desk, a three-drawer cabinet, a chair, shelving on the wall above the desk, a lamp and an ashtray, and all of it without the faintest connection whatsoever to anyone or anywhere or anything else in my life.

I went to the first-floor window and looked out at the empty playing fields beneath me and the unfamiliar streets beyond. I put my bag in the wardrobe, the cigarettes on the desk and the bottle of whisky on the shelving – anything to announce my presence in that empty, silent space. I sat on the bed, lit a cigarette and listened to the voices, footsteps and the banging of cases in the corridor outside. I went from the bed to the chair, took down the bottle of whisky, unscrewed the cap, sniffed it and then started to consider where I might find a glass to pour myself a drink.